A CURIOUS COLLECTION

OF

PECULIAR CREATURES

AN ILLUSTRATED ENCYCLOPEDIA

SAMI BAYLY

THE EXPERIMENT

NEW YORK

CONTENTS

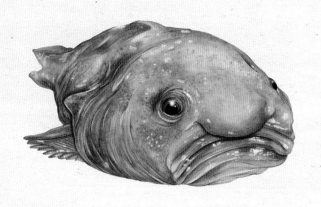

INTRODUCTION

A Curious Collection of Peculiar Creatures *is a celebration of the beauty in the, well, less conventionally beautiful animals of our planet.* While painting these sixty animals in scientific detail, I came to reject our contemporary standards of appearance, finding them unfair and, really, missing the point. Regarding these animals' more otherworldly attributes, the ones some may call "unseemly"—such as the giant anteater's astonishingly long snout, or the blobfish's general blobbiness—I'd like to make the case for celebrating them as "ingenious," even "refined"; they almost always play a key role, exquisitely adapted over many years, for survival.

It's long overdue for these weird and wonderful species to have their turn to shine: Their survival—and ours—may depend on it. That's because, in spite of all their miraculous abilities, they're no match for humans' capacity for destruction. Through my research, I realized how many were endangered—and how, without them, our amazing and diverse ecosystems would cease to function.

I hope that by the end of this book, you will find your perception of beauty challenged and learn something new to tell your family and friends—and, most importantly, find a peculiar creature to love.

AMAZON RIVER DOLPHIN

Inia geoffrensis

(in-e-a geo-fren-sis)

W hy are Amazon River dolphins pink? It's something of a mystery. Like other dolphins, they're born grey, but they become pinker as they get older, and males are usually pinker than females. Their mottled grey-and-pink coloring may help them blend into the muddy waters of their surroundings. Or the pink may be scar tissue that the males develop over years of fights and scrapes with other dolphins. Either way, the pinker the male, the more popular he'll be with females.

The dolphins use the large bulge on their heads—called a melon—for echolocation: It sends out clicking sounds through the water that bounce back when they hit something. The melon processes the returning sounds, helping the dolphins figure out the size and location of potential prey without having to see it. And they can safely wend their way through the murky waters of the Amazon thanks to their chubby, flexible necks, which allow them to turn their heads up to 90 degrees in any direction! These tubby freshwater mammals can reach a length of 8 feet (2.5 m) for males and 6 feet (2 m) for females.

Where They Live

Like their name suggests, these dolphins live in the Amazon River, which runs through the South American countries of Brazil, Colombia, and Peru. They can also be found in the Orinoco River, which flows through Colombia and Venezuela, and sometimes they even turn up in rivers in Bolivia and Ecuador. They enjoy swimming in tropical rivers, ponds, and lakes, and also spend time in forested areas that flood during the rainy season.

What They Eat

These dolphins survive on any species of fish they can find near the riverbed, but they'll also use their sharp teeth to eat turtles, crabs, and even the toothy piranha!

Conservation Status

NOT ENOUGH DATA

There's a lot we don't understand about the Amazon River dolphin— exactly how many there are, where they live, whether they're endangered. They're said to be abundant in some regions, but in others they may struggle to survive. What we do know is that humans are a threat. Sometimes fishermen accidentally catch them or destroy their habitat with netting. Sometimes they're caught to use as bait or deliberately killed because they eat fish the fishermen want to catch. And some live in rivers where people practice explosive fishing, which involves throwing bombs into the water to kill fish, harming the dolphins. Local peoples are reluctant to hunt the Amazon river dolphin and will only use the body parts of a dolphin that's already died. When this happens, they use the dolphin's fat and oil for medicinal remedies, and their teeth and eyes as love charms.

AMERICAN MANATEE

Trichechus manatus
(tri-kek-us man-a-tus)

With their pudgy, hairy bodies, paddle-shaped flippers, and wrinkly, grey skin covered in algae, these docile, slow-moving sea cows may appear to have missed out in the beauty department. But all of these so-called misfortunes are actually adaptations that make manatees better suited to their environment. Their paddle-shaped limbs help propel them along the seafloor so they use less energy while traveling and feeding, and their drab-colored skin helps them blend into their environment, protecting them from predators.

The bristly hairs on their bodies and around their mouths pick up vibrations in the water that give them information about their surroundings. American manatees rely on this adaptation because of their poor eyesight. These massive mammals can reach up to 8 feet (2.5 m) long and weigh in at an average of 440 to 1,320 pounds (200–600 kg).

Where They Live

You'll find the American manatee in the United States, mainly in Florida and Georgia, and sometimes farther south, in countries such as Mexico and the Bahamas. Like other migratory animals, manatees travel to find warmer water as the seasons change. They live in channels, canals, creeks, lagoons, and seagrass beds, at shallow depths ranging from 1.5 to 20 feet (0.5–6 m).

What They Eat

American manatees eat seagrasses, algae, roots, and mangrove leaves. But they don't have hands or fingers, so how do they pluck plants to eat? Well, they have very unusual upper lips! These are divided into two halves that can move independently of each other, which allows the manatee to grasp individual plants to snack on. The manatee doesn't have front teeth—only some molars at the back of the jaw. These molars become worn down easily, but are replaced by new ones throughout the animal's lifetime.

Close Relations

Although manatees live in the water, they're most closely related to another large, grey, wrinkly mammal that lives on land—the elephant! If you look carefully, you'll see they have three or four tiny nails at the end of each flipper, much like an elephant's toenails.

Conservation Status

VULNERABLE

Humans are the biggest threat facing the American manatee. These marine mammals tend to live in shallow water and are very large, so they're frequently struck by boats. They're also hunted for their skin and bones.

FUN FACTS

✳ American manatees can eat for up to 8 hours a day, consuming an average of 70 pounds (30 kg) of food. That's a lot of seagrass!

✳ Pirates would eat dried manatee meat, called buccan, so often that they became known as buccaneers.

✳ Manatees spend their entire lives in the water, but since they're mammals, they have to hold their breath while they're submerged—just like us! They usually stay underwater for around 4 minutes, but they can go for as long as 18 minutes before coming up for air.

✳ Even though manatees don't have long, flowing hair or shimmering blue tails, colonist and explorer Christopher Columbus believed he was looking at the mythical mermaid when he first saw them.

ANTARCTIC SCALE WORM

Eulagisca gigantea

(yool-a-gis-ka gi-gant-e-a)

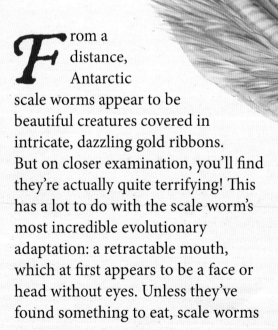

From a distance, Antarctic scale worms appear to be beautiful creatures covered in intricate, dazzling gold ribbons. But on closer examination, you'll find they're actually quite terrifying! This has a lot to do with the scale worm's most incredible evolutionary adaptation: a retractable mouth, which at first appears to be a face or head without eyes. Unless they've found something to eat, scale worms always keep their mouths tucked inside their bodies, out of sight.

These 8-inch-long (20 cm) marine worms belong to a group called polychaetes, more commonly known as bristle worms. No one knows exactly what purpose the brush-like bristles on their sides serve, but they may help scale worms defend themselves against predators. Or they may help the worms move across seabeds, or even help them swim.

Where They Live

Finding a scale worm isn't easy. They live deep in the Southern Ocean near Antarctica, sometimes keeping warm in the heated water that flows out of hydrothermal vents— openings in the seafloor found near underwater volcanoes.

What They Eat

We don't know much about what scale worms eat or how they feed themselves. Scientists assume they eat other deep-sea animals, but no one knows exactly which ones. They have a large mouth and teeth, which suggests they're quick and aggressive hunters. Fortunately, they pose no threat to humans—we can't even reach the deep-sea waters they live in unless we're in heavily protected equipment, like submarines!

Conservation Status

NOT EVALUATED

Scientists know very little about the scale worm's conservation status or the potential threats to its survival. But since they live in the deep sea, like blobfish and batfish (pages 34 and 96), scale worms are probably endangered by similar threats, such as trawling or shifts in water temperature caused by climate change.

FUN FACTS

* The tooth-like scales that cover the scale worm's body are known as elytra.

* Scale worms were first discovered in 1939, when they were added to the World Register of Marine Species (WoRMS), but not much has been documented about them since then.

* Their class, Polychaeta, means "many bristles" in Latin.

* The collective name for a group of worms is a bed.

* Scale worms were discovered quite recently. Some scientists believe there could be around 16,000 undiscovered species of marine worms! We only know of about 8,000 species right now.

ASIAN SHEEPSHEAD WRASSE

Semicossyphus reticulatus

(semi-kos-e-fus re-tik-you-la-tus)

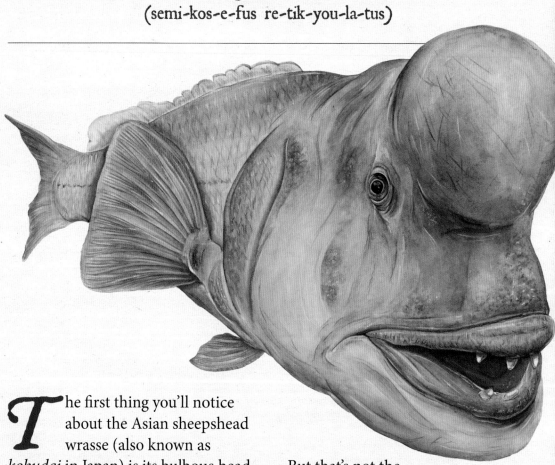

The first thing you'll notice about the Asian sheepshead wrasse (also known as *kobudai* in Japan) is its bulbous head and chin. We don't know much about the purpose of these impressive bony growths, which appear only on males, but they might be useful in attracting females during breeding season.

But that's not the most amazing thing about this fish: A female wrasse can transform into a male halfway through her life! Scientists don't fully understand why this happens, but they believe it may be a way for the fish to produce more offspring.

The male sheepshead wrasse can reach a massive 3 feet (1 m) long and can weigh up to 32 pounds (14.5 kg). Females are much smaller (before they turn into males, that is!).

Where They Live

Asian sheepshead wrasse live in the cool seas surrounding Japan, China, and North and South Korea, where they're especially fond of rocky reefs.

What They Eat

Scientists believe this wrasse mainly eats crustaceans and shellfish. This would explain their unusual teeth, which are perfectly designed for chewing through and opening shells.

Conservation Status

NOT ENOUGH DATA

Unfortunately, there isn't much information about this species of wrasse, but we do know their population is dwindling. Overfishing will probably endanger them if no limitations are put in place. The wrasse is also threatened by many chemicals we use to clean our houses. When we pour these down the drain, they can end up in the ocean and may harm the fish's ability to reproduce.

FUN FACTS

* Animals that can change genders, whether from male to female or from female to male, are called sequential hermaphrodites. There aren't many creatures that can do this, though—just certain kinds of fish, snails, and slugs.

* It's difficult to collect data about this species thanks to its gender-fluid ways. A fish that's recorded as female one day may become male by the next time it's studied.

* When wrasse that were born female change into males, they can grow even larger than wrasse that were born male.

ATLANTIC MUDSKIPPER

Periophthalmus barbarus
(peer-e-off-thal-mus bar-ba-rus)

This territorial, amphibious fish is quite the looker. Their brown, slimy body can reach 6 inches (15 cm) long. Their eyes sit on top of their head, rather than on the sides, which makes them look a little like a frog—and means they have a 360-degree view of the world.

The mudskipper's pectoral fins—the ones on their chest, closest to their head—are shaped like limbs and let the fish "walk" over rocks and sand. Mudskippers have even been known to climb up the roots of mangrove trees!

They get their name from their long, strong tail, which they can use as a springboard to propel themselves forward in a skipping or hopping motion. This clever adaptation not only helps them escape predators, but also lets them get around on land.

But the most remarkable thing about this fish? They spend most of their time on land! Incredibly, the Atlantic mudskipper has evolved to live both in and out of the water. They can even breathe in the air thanks to small pockets behind their gills where water and oxygen are stored.

Where They Live

Atlantic mudskippers are found along the coast of West Africa and off islands in the Gulf of Guinea. They prefer shallow, muddy, swampy areas where they can spend their days darting back and forth between the water and land, keeping themselves hydrated while searching for food.

What They Eat

Since mudskippers are able to hunt for food both underwater and on land, they can be found feasting on all sorts of creatures, including crickets, flies, beetles, worms, small fish, and crabs.

Conservation Status

LEAST CONCERN

Fortunately, Atlantic mudskippers are under very little threat from humans or other predators. They also have a large, widespread habitat range, which means they can make their homes in many places.

FUN FACTS

✴ When they're on land, Atlantic mudskippers keep their eyes wet by rolling them down into pockets filled with water located beneath their eyes.

✴ During mating season, the males become more vibrant in color.

✴ Males that live close to one another are quite competitive about their territory and will act aggressively toward each other, sometimes fighting to the death.

✴ There are 15 species of mudskipper in the world; the Atlantic mudskipper has the largest population of them all.

✴ Their scientific name, *Periophthalmus*, refers to their ability to see all around them, in every direction, and translates to "round eye."

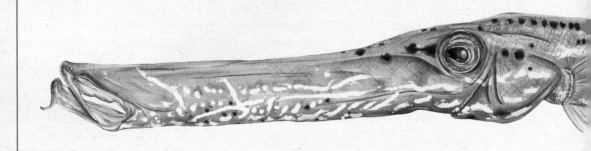

ATLANTIC TRUMPETFISH

Aulostomus strigosus

(awl-os-toe-mus strig-o-sus)

The Atlantic trumpetfish is a true camouflage artist, which comes in handy both when hiding from predators and hunting for food. They're able to catch unsuspecting prey by changing color—from brown to yellow to blue to purple—to blend in with the reefs that make up their home.

But that's not their only trick! The trumpetfish has a long, thin body that looks a lot like seagrass or coral and can reach a length of 3 feet (1 m). They'll spend hours floating vertically with their head pointed down toward the seafloor, pretending to be a harmless piece of seagrass until a meal shows up.

If predators do catch sight of them, trumpetfish have spines down their back, which they can raise to help defend themselves.

Where They Live

Atlantic trumpetfish like to swim at depths of around 13 to 80 feet (4–25 m), in clear waters surrounded by coral and reefs. They live in the western Atlantic Ocean—around south Florida, the Bahamas, the Gulf of Mexico, and Bermuda.

What They Eat

The trumpetfish may seem to have a long mouth, but what you're seeing is really a very long *face*, or snout! Their mouths are actually quite small. They hunt by waiting until the very last moment before pouncing on their prey and thrusting their mouths forward to suction up the unsuspecting meal, which is usually made up of small invertebrates or fish. Tasty!

Close Relations

Like seahorses, which they're related to, male Atlantic trumpetfish carry and care for their eggs in a small pouch until they're ready to hatch.

Conservation Status

LEAST CONCERN

From a conservation perspective, the Atlantic trumpetfish is considered of least concern, but that doesn't mean it's always been safe or always will be. In the 1970s, the species lost a large portion of its habitat because of large-scale coral loss caused by humans. Measures are currently in place to protect this fish, but it's important to be aware that our actions can have devastating effects on the world around us.

FUN FACTS

✳ Atlantic trumpetfish get their name from their long snouts, which resemble trumpets. Sometimes they're also called the painted flutemouth.

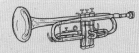

✳ Male trumpetfish win over females by performing an elaborate mating dance during which they change colors several times!

✳ Invasive lionfish are a major threat to the survival of the Atlantic trumpetfish because of the destruction they cause to native sea plants and corals.

AUSTRALIAN BRUSH-TURKEY

Alectura lathami

(a-lek-tura la-tha-me)

L ike other turkeys, these big, colorful birds sport an unflattering wrinkled pouch around their neck, known as a wattle. The wattles are much larger in the males—turkeys are a sexually dimorphic bird, which means that males and females have different physical features, making it easy to tell them apart. The brush-turkey's wattle is usually yellow, but it can vary in color based on the turkey's habitat and age. In North Queensland in Australia, for instance, their wattles tend to be pale blue.

These turkeys have large, powerful feet and claws that let them dig up the earth. They are one of the megapodes, a group of around 22 fowl-like birds that are known for their large feet.

Where They Live

Like their name suggests, the Australian brush-turkey can be found in Australia, from New South Wales to Far North Queensland. They live in shrub-like environments, rain forests, and other forested coastal places.

What They Eat

Using their powerful feet, brush-turkeys search under the earth for food like insects, fruit, and seeds. Unfortunately, this method of foraging has made them a very unpopular bird in rural Australia, as they will often visit neatly kept gardens and destroy them in just one short feeding session.

Close Relations

They are related to the wild turkey (page 124).

Conservation Status

LEAST CONCERN

Experts believe there are more than 100,000 individual brush-turkeys, and their numbers are currently very strong. This is good news, since they became very rare after the Great Depression of the 1930s, when Australians hunted them for food and took their eggs to eat. Today, the main threats to the brush-turkey population are foxes and cats; goanna lizards, which eat their eggs; and humans, who encroach on their habitat.

FUN FACTS

✳ Male brush-turkeys build mound-like nests to attract females, and sometimes their nests are as large as a car!

✳ If you'd like to keep a brush-turkey out of your yard, you'd better hide any food left outside for your pets—they'll think it's for them and happily make a meal of it.

✳ Brush-turkey chicks can care for themselves and are even able to fly only a few hours after hatching.

✳ Standing around 2 feet (60 cm) tall and weighing roughly 5 pounds (2 kg), the Australian brush-turkey is the largest of all the megapodes.

✳ Their family, the Megapodiidae, dates back 30 million years.

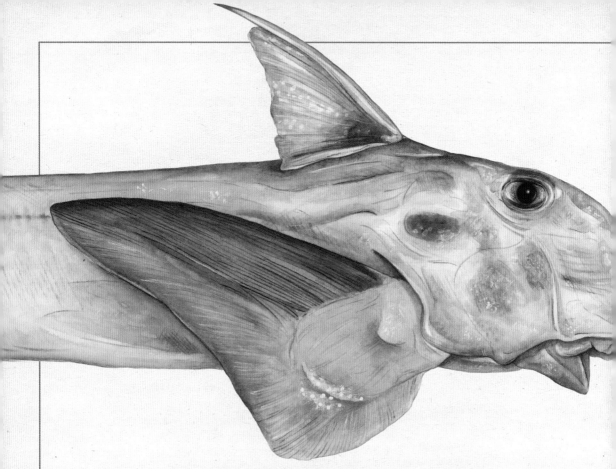

AUSTRALIAN GHOST SHARK

Callorhinchus milii

(kal-or-ink-us mil-e-eye)

*T*he small, silver Australian ghost shark is a mysterious creature. They aren't true sharks, but they aren't true fish, either. Instead, they're chimaera, and they're only distantly related to sharks and rays. This ghost shark goes by many names: the elephant fish, the whitefish, the plownose chimaera. All of them refer to the distinctive adaptations the species

has developed over time—especially their long, large, strangely shaped snouts, which are coated in sensory pores called electroreceptors that detect electrical fields and movement. This helps the ghost shark find prey buried under layers of sand and dirt.

Where They Live

You'll find these unusual creatures swimming in estuaries and shallow coastal waters off South Australia and New Zealand when they're young. When they're older, they travel to much deeper waters—up to 655 feet (200 m) deep!

What They Eat

Ghost sharks are carnivorous and use their trunk-like nose to plow through sandy ocean floors in search of food, including other fish, mollusks, clams, worms, and shellfish.

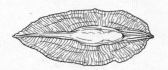

Conservation Status

LEAST CONCERN

Although they're regularly farmed by humans and are also hunted by larger ocean-dwelling predators such as true sharks, the Australian ghost shark isn't at grave risk of extinction.

Due to overfishing in Australian waters, limitations have been put in place to try to prevent any further drop in the ghost shark's numbers. In Victoria, for example, you're allowed to catch only one per day.

But it's not just fishing that has a negative impact on the ghost shark: The equipment used to retrieve them from the water often destroys the surrounding environment.

Ghost sharks can fall victim to parasites that can cause physical damage and harm their ability to reproduce.

FUN FACTS

✳ You may have eaten a ghost shark for dinner! In both New Zealand and Australia, they're often served in fish and chips.

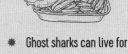

✳ Ghost sharks can live for up to 15 years.

✳ Their eggs, which take eight months to hatch, are nothing like bird's eggs! They have a leathery texture and can measure 10 inches (25 cm) long.

✳ Like sharks, their skeleton is made of cartilage rather than bone.

AUSTRALIAN WHITE IBIS

Threskiornis moluccus

(thres-key-or-nis mol-uk-us)

Most of the body is covered in fluffy white feathers, but the head of the Australian white ibis is bald and black. This makes for a striking contrast, but it serves a practical purpose too: Without feathers on their head and neck, these birds have an easy time grooming themselves after eating messy meals, and they're less likely to get sick from mites or other pests.

There are red patches of skin on the back of their neck and the underside of their wings, and these become more vibrant during breeding season. Unfortunately, these birds have lost much of their natural habitat to humans, forcing them to live in dirty, polluted environments where their beautiful white plumage quickly becomes brown and soiled.

Where They Live

The Australian white ibis used to inhabit wetlands throughout Queensland and all the way down to Victoria. But much of their habitat has been destroyed to make way for human expansion, and these birds tend to live in heavily populated urban environments now.

What They Eat

Ibis beaks are incredible tools, designed for catching creatures like insects and mussels that live in holes or tunnels and for hammering shells against hard rocks to crack them open. These days, though, you're more likely to see these birds using their beaks to reach into a trash bin and pull out food scraps. As humans have encroached on their natural habitat, the Australian white ibis has learned to scavenge from landfills and trash heaps.

Close Relations

As you can probably tell from their name, these birds are closely related to the northern bald ibis (page 86). Not only are they both ibis, but they both have hairless heads and long, thin beaks.

Conservation Status

LEAST CONCERN

The Australian white ibis faces tremendous threats such as habitat loss, hunting, and the general effects of a poor diet. Approximately 50 percent of these birds eat from landfills every day. Nevertheless, their numbers are stable, and they're not considered to be threatened.

FUN FACTS

* If you live in Australia, you may have heard these birds called by other names, such as "bin chicken," "trash turkey," or "flying rat," because of their habit of eating from trash bins and landfills.

* During courtship, the male performs a noisy routine to entice the female. He will then gift her a small twig, and the two will groom one another. How romantic!

* Certain local governments across Australia have permits to hunt the birds because they're seen as pests.

* Approximately 9,000 ibis were counted in Sydney in 2014.

AYE-AYE

Daubentonia madagascariensis

(doo-ben-toe-ne-a ma-da-gas-kar-e-en-sis)

Aye-ayes have enormous ears and a piercing gaze. Their front teeth are long and sharp, and they have a strange extended third finger. Ugly as they may be, each of these features serves a purpose.

Since they're nocturnal, these primates have developed wide-set eyes for clearer vision in the dark. And they use their giant ears in an unusual way when looking for food: They cup them around tree trunks and branches while tapping their elongated fingers quickly against the wood. This way, they're able to hear where hollow spaces are. Then they use their teeth to gnaw holes in the bark, stretch their long middle fingers into the holes, and pierce grubs and insects with their hook-like nail, dragging them out to eat. This method of finding food is called percussive foraging, and aye-ayes are one of only a few species to use it.

Where They Live

Found along the coasts of Madagascar, the aye-aye likes to live in forests and coconut plantations, as well as in swampy stands of mangroves. During the day, they hide up in the tree canopy, but they're active at night, spending the safe hours of darkness hunting for food in the treetops.

What They Eat

The aye-aye uses its elongated finger to scoop out nectar and insects from coconuts and trees. Most of their diet is made up of tree cankers (growths on tree bark caused by fungi or bacteria), fruit, nectar, and large quantities of insect larvae, which provide protein and fat.

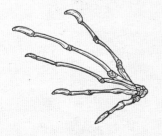

Close Relations

While these small animals might look like rodents, they're actually primates and are related to apes and chimpanzees.

Conservation Status

ENDANGERED

According to local superstition in Madagascar, the aye-aye is a sign of bad luck or even death, and many people believe that if one points at you with its long middle finger, you'll die. Unfortunately, this means that humans are the greatest threat to the aye-aye's survival. They're often killed if they're spotted during the night, then hung by their tails along the roadside so passersby will take the bad luck with them as they leave. Another threat to the aye-aye's survival is habitat loss, as trees and land are cleared to provide lumber for houses, boats, and other uses.

FUN FACTS

✳ Aye-ayes have the largest brains among the prosimians, a group of many different primate species that also includes lemurs.

✳ Their name may come from the sound they make when startled: "hai-hai."

✳ They've lived as long as 23 years in captivity.

BALD-HEADED UAKARI

Cacajao calvus
(ca-ka-jow cal-vus)

The bald-headed uakari's bright red face and hairless head may look strange to humans, but to other uakaris, they're very attractive! Crimson cheeks signal health and appeal to potential mates. A pale complexion is a turnoff, as it implies sickness or even a malaria infection, which is common among the species.

Uakaris are smart, playful, communal monkeys. They frequently express their emotions and thoughts through facial expressions and sounds.

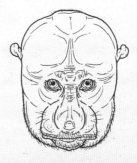

Where They Live

Bald-headed uakaris are found in the forests of Brazil and Peru, in low-density areas near water sources. They're arboreal monkeys, so they feel safer in the treetops, but they'll come down to the ground from time to time. They can be spotted more easily than other monkeys because of their vibrant coloring.

What They Eat

Usually, uakaris eat high up in trees, where they feed on leaves, nuts, fruit, and insects. Occasionally they'll climb down to the forest floor to feast on dropped fruits and seeds. They split up to find food during the day, then gather together at night to sleep in groups—safety in numbers!

Conservation Status

VULNERABLE

Bald-headed uakaris are regularly hunted for food by humans and also face habitat loss, which makes the species vulnerable. Deforestation is especially threatening to them because the trees are their home.

FUN FACTS

❋ The collective name for a group of uakaris is a troop.

❋ The correct way to pronounce their name is "wakari."

❋ They give birth to one infant only once every two years.

❋ Their tails are small and stumpy, so they rely on their arms and legs to move through the tree branches.

❋ Their faces are red because they have only a thin layer of skin covering their capillaries. The color you can see is actually flowing blood!

BLACK MUSSELCRACKER

Cymatoceps nasutus

(sym-a-toe-seps nay-suh-tus)

This is not your ordinary small coral fish. Black musselcrackers are gigantic! They can reach 4 feet (130 cm) long and weigh up to 99 pounds (45 kg).

Their plump, nose-like snouts make them look quite human, and their mouth is full of powerful teeth. These teeth are how they got the name "musselcracker."

Like the Asian sheepshead wrasse (page 12), they're able to change from female to male. This unusual ability is known as hermaphroditism, and it usually occurs when females reach maturity, around 18 years of age and 2 feet (70 cm) long.

Scientists have various theories to explain why this happens, but it's probably a way to make sure the species will continue to reproduce even when there aren't many available males.

Where They Live

Found in the waters off South Africa and Mozambique, the adults reside in rocky reef environments approximately 330 feet (100 m) deep, while the young prefer shallow homes in rock pools or ditches. They favor warm, clear waters and are quite sensitive to changes in water temperature.

What They Eat

Foods that appeal to the black musselcracker include crustaceans and mollusks, such as starfish, crabs, sea urchins, and other creatures with a hard shell or surface. These fish have very strong jaws and can use their molars and front teeth to crack the shells of their prey and consume the insides.

Conservation Status

VULNERABLE

Unfortunately, black musselcrackers are considered trophy fish, and they're being overfished, which means their population is diminishing. Fishing limitations have been put in place to keep their numbers up: You can catch only one musselcracker per day, and if it's less than 20 inches (50 cm) long, you have to release it.

FUN FACTS

* Their scientific name, *Cymatoceps nasutus*, translates from Latin to "swollen head" and "prominent nose."

* They can live for a long time— as long as 45 years!

* In Afrikaans, their name is *poenskop*.

* Parts of the black musselcracker are considered a delicacy in some areas of the world, meaning their catch rate is quite high.

* The larger this fish grows, the more human its face looks!

BLACK RAIN FROG

Breviceps fuscus

(brev-e-seps fuss-cus)

Black rain frogs are very small, only about 1.5 to 2 inches (4–5 cm) long. However, when they're feeling threatened or scared, they'll puff themselves up to seem much larger and more menacing. With their sad expressions and knobby skin, this makes them look a little like a bumpy, grumpy balloon! But it's all part of their defense mechanism.

Doing this may frighten off a hungry snake or pig. It also keeps them safe from being pulled out of their burrows by predators—once they're puffed up, they can't fit through the entrance!

Where They Live

To find this species, you have to travel to South Africa, particularly the forests and heathland areas of the southernmost tip, known as the Cape Fold Mountains. Since these are burrowing frogs, you won't find them spending their days in water! Instead, they hang out in tunnels up to 6 inches (15 cm) deep, in the slopes and hills around the mountains. These frogs are nocturnal, so they're active only at night.

What They Eat

No one knows exactly what black rain frogs eat. Most likely, they spend their time hunting worms, spiders, and insects, which they then slurp up with their sticky tongues.

Conservation Status

LEAST CONCERN

Black rain frogs are hunted by predators like pigs, snakes, and birds of prey, and they're also threatened by environmental changes. Invasive plant species and frequent wildfires put their habitat at risk. Fortunately, scientists are monitoring these issues to make sure the frogs' numbers don't fall too low.

FUN FACTS

* A group of black rain frogs is called an army or a knot.

* Black rain frogs can be very clever. The females lay around 43 eggs in their burrow. Then they lay another set of eggs on top—but these eggs are empty! This way, when predators raid the burrows to eat the eggs, the ones with babies in them are more likely to survive.

* When these frogs mate, the female makes a sticky goo that keeps the male attached to her for as long as it takes to fertilize the eggs—and sometimes even longer!

* The male frogs keep watch over the eggs while waiting for them to hatch.

BLACK SNUB-NOSED MONKEY

Rhinopithecus bieti

(ry-nop-ith-e-kus by-e-ti)

*T*hese monkeys look especially unusual because of their upturned nose and plump, rosy lips. Their nose doesn't have a nasal bone, and their big lips cover large gums and teeth, which they display when feeling threatened or scared.

The males weigh in at a rather hefty average of 31 pounds (14 kg) and can reach lengths of 3 to 5 feet (100–155 cm), including their tail. Females are smaller, measuring just over half the size of males.

These monkeys use a range of calls and alarms to communicate with each other, including lighthearted cheeps to show playfulness and barking to indicate rage, as well as a number of calls to warn of oncoming danger.

Where They Live

The black snub-nosed monkey can be found in southwestern China, in a region called Yunnan. In fact, they're sometimes called the Yunnan snub-nosed monkey. They live in forests around 2.5 miles (4,000 m) above sea level, where it's snowy almost every day of the year!

What They Eat

Black snub-nosed monkeys rely on fungus, algae, bamboo, and the lichen on trees to give them energy throughout the day. In springtime, they also eat berries, insects, grass, and flowers.

Conservation Status

ENDANGERED

This is yet another unique primate that's struggling to survive because of overwhelming deforestation, poaching, and the impact of climate change on its habitat. Since the early 1980s, their numbers have fallen by 31 percent. On top of this, black snub-nosed monkeys are frequently poisoned or caught in snares put down for other animals. People are trying to help them survive by running breeding programs in China, funding protected areas where they can live safely, and promoting awareness about their plight.

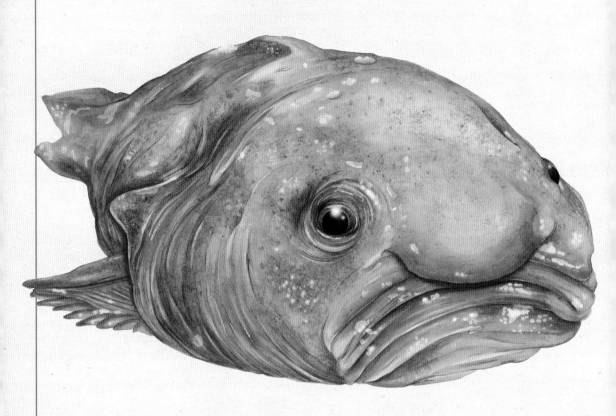

BLOBFISH

Psychrolutes microporos
(sy-kro-loots mi-cro-pore-os)

This soft, droopy-faced fish has evolved to survive under very strong water pressure, which is why it looks a little like a blob. It doesn't have much need for muscles or bones, since the depths where it lives can be 120 times the pressure at sea level. Even though the blobfish looks odd to us, it's perfectly adapted to its environment. It weighs around 4 pounds (2 kg) and can reach around 1 foot (30 cm) in length.

Where They Live

The blobfish lives in the Indian, Pacific, and Atlantic Oceans, at depths two and a half times deeper than most submarines can reach! The first specimen was found off the coast of New Zealand in 2003 by a scientific research team of Australians and New Zealanders. It was discovered 4,265 feet (1,300 m) beneath the surface.

What They Eat

Since they must save their minimal energy for daily tasks, the blobfish probably feeds on other slow-moving prey, such as sea snails, slugs, urchins, and mollusks.

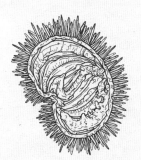

Close Relations

This fish is part of the Psychrolutidae family, which also includes the toadfish.

Conservation Status

NOT EVALUATED

The blobfish was discovered only recently, and scientists know very little about it. Given the environment it lives in, it probably has few predators and threats. Humans pose the greatest risk to the blobfish, because of deep-sea trawling nets as well as climate change, which causes shifts in the oceans' temperature.

FUN FACTS

✳ Blobfish can live an incredibly long time—as long as 130 years! This could be because deep-sea creatures tend to age very slowly, and because of their lack of predators.

✳ The first specimen ever found was given to the Australian Museum, where it's known as "Mr. Blobby" and is now preserved and on display for educational purposes.

✳ Like the ocean sunfish (page 90)—but unlike most other fish—blobfish don't have a swim bladder to help them float. Instead, they rely on their jelly-like flesh for buoyancy.

✳ In 2013, the blobfish was voted the world's ugliest animal by the Ugly Animal Preservation Society.

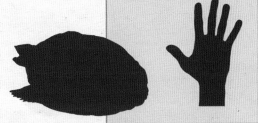

BORNEAN ORANGUTAN

Pongo pygmaeus
(pong-go pig-may-us)

These primates are certainly not the most beautiful animals in the world, but their faces are unforgettable!

Males have large cheek pads (known as flanges) on each side of their face, giving their head a round, dinner-plate-like appearance. No one knows exactly what purpose these serve, although researchers have noted that the larger the flanges, the more attractive a male will be to females.

The Bornean orangutan can weigh 130 to 200 pounds (60–90 kg) and grow to 3 feet (90 cm) tall. They have remarkably long arms that can measure up to 3 feet (90 cm) long! These help them swing from tree to tree.

Where They Live

To see Bornean orangutans in the wild, you'll have to visit the hilly forest zones in the Kalimantan, Sabah, and Sarawak regions of Borneo (an island in the southwestern Pacific Ocean). Every night, they build nests high in the trees to sleep in, safe from the reach of predators.

What They Eat

Bornean orangutans use their opposable thumbs to pick their food, and they sip water from rain caught in cupped leaves. Their diet consists mostly of plants, fruits, and flowers, though they also eat a range of insects and will sometimes feed on small mammals.

Conservation Status

CRITICALLY ENDANGERED

The Bornean orangutan's numbers are dropping quickly because of massive habitat loss and poaching. Each year, thousands of them are killed in the Kalimantan region of Borneo alone, mostly for food, and approximately 82 percent of the population has been lost since the 1940s. To make matters worse, Bornean orangutans need a long time to reproduce. So it's no surprise, sadly, that they're critically endangered.

FUN FACTS

* Bornean orangutans can live as long as 60 years.

* The word *orangutan* translates to "man of the forest" in Malay and Indonesian.

* Although they live on an island, you won't find Bornean orangutans playing in the ocean: They can't swim!

* Humans share 97 percent of their DNA with these primates.

* They are the largest tree-dwelling mammals in the world!

CALIFORNIA CONDOR

Gymnogyps californianus

(gym-no-gips ka-li-forn-e-a-nus)

California condors are tremendous birds! They have a wingspan of up to 10 feet (3 m) and can weigh as much as 30 pounds (14 kg). The males are typically larger than the females but have similar colors: glossy black feathers with striking white patches under their wings.

Their pink, wrinkly, featherless heads may detract a bit from their looks, but since they're scavengers that feed on carcasses, a bald head is a useful adaptation—it keeps them safe from contracting parasites or infections after a messy meal of rotting meat.

Where They Live

The California condor once occupied the entire length of the Pacific coast of North America, but now they can be found only in south-central California. They enjoy living in rocky cliffs and tall trees. These high perches allow them to survey the area for food and are also safe spots to build nests for their young.

What They Eat

California condors feast on carrion, which means they're mostly carnivorous but generally won't kill their food themselves. Instead, they flock to creatures such as cattle, deer, and rabbits that have already been killed by cars or other animals, or that have died naturally. They eat approximately 3 pounds (1.5 kg) of meat a day! Their love of carrion helps hurry along the process of decomposition and rids the area of germs, making scavenger birds like this condor crucial to the health of the ecosystem.

Conservation Status

CRITICALLY ENDANGERED

The California condor is critically endangered for several reasons, including widespread hunting and habitat destruction. They are especially vulnerable to accidental lead poisoning, which happens when the birds eat dead animals that farmers and local hunters have shot with lead bullets.

FUN FACTS

* California condors will consume so much food in one meal that they can't fly for a few hours afterward.

* They have been recorded to live for as long as 60 years.

* They're superb gliders and can soar on the wind for up to an hour without needing to flap their wings even once.

* The California condor is the biggest bird in all of North America!

* Like many other birds, they mate for life.

CHINESE SOFTSHELL TURTLE

Pelodiscus sinensis

(pel-o-dis-kus si-nen-sis)

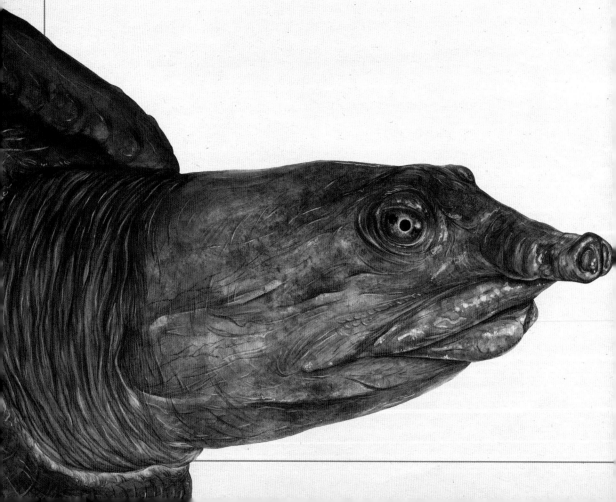

As their name suggests, the Chinese softshell turtle has a soft, smooth, leathery shell, which makes them truly unusual—most turtles have very hard, knobby shells. Since they spend most of their time in the water, their feet are webbed to make swimming easier. They also sport a long snout with nostrils at the very end, which they can use like a snorkel to breathe even when underwater or buried in mud.

This species of turtle is sexually dimorphic—the female is larger than the male, reaching around 1 foot (30 cm) long and weighing up to 13 pounds (6 kg), and her blotchy, dark-olive shell has a more pronounced curve than the male's.

Where They Live

Like most turtles, Chinese softshells love to inhabit the fresh and brackish waters of rivers, swamps, creeks, and lakes. They are native to China and Southeast Asia but have been introduced to other pockets of Asia, too.

What They Eat

These turtles are mostly carnivorous, preferring to dine on small creatures like insects, worms, fish, and crustaceans. They'll also eat leaves and aquatic vegetation.

Conservation Status

VULNERABLE

The Chinese softshell turtle's numbers have decreased over time, and the species is now listed as vulnerable. Various factors have contributed to their slow decline, but the main cause is human exploitation. Softshell turtles are farmed and hunted in China for their meat.

FUN FACTS

✳ Although their shells are called "soft," they're not completely soft! A solid bone in the middle helps the structure remain rigid while still being flexible.

✳ Researchers aren't sure exactly how long these turtles live, but they seem to reach adulthood when they're around four to six years old.

✳ The Chinese softshell turtle is incredibly important to the Asian economy—millions of them are bred and sold for food each year.

✳ Like birds, baby turtles hatch from eggs. Several times each year, female turtles lay between 8 and 30 eggs in a nest. It generally takes 60 days for the eggs to hatch, but this depends on the weather and temperature of the surrounding environment.

CREATONOTOS GANGIS

Creatonotos gangis

(cree-a-ton-oat-os gang-gis)

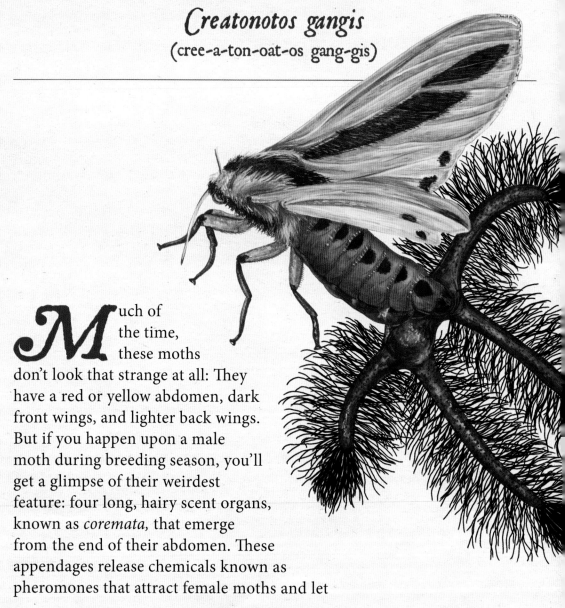

Much of the time, these moths don't look that strange at all: They have a red or yellow abdomen, dark front wings, and lighter back wings. But if you happen upon a male moth during breeding season, you'll get a glimpse of their weirdest feature: four long, hairy scent organs, known as *coremata*, that emerge from the end of their abdomen. These appendages release chemicals known as pheromones that attract female moths and let them know the males are ready to mate. When fully extended, the coremata are longer than the moth's entire body, which can be up to 1.5 inches (4 cm) long.

Where They Live

Keep an eye out for the *Creatonotos gangis* if you're out and about in Southeast Asia—including India, Sri Lanka, Thailand, and parts of Indonesia—or if you're roaming around Australia's Northern Territory, Western Australia, or Queensland.

What They Eat

This moth's diet is also highly unusual. As a caterpillar, and sometimes as a moth too, the *Creatonotos gangis* loves to eat plants that produce chemicals called pyrrolizidine alkaloids (PAs)—such as pomegranate trees, rice, soybeans, and corn. These chemicals are foul-tasting and toxic, and they drive away almost all other insects and animals! But for *Creatonotos gangis*, PAs are not just a delicious snack—they also help the moths grow their gangly coremata. The more PAs the caterpillars eat, the larger their coremata will be when they become moths. And the larger their coremata, the better chance they'll have to reproduce.

Conservation Status

NOT EVALUATED

Very little is known about the conservation status of the *Creatonotos gangis*. Hopefully, more research will be done on these moths in the future so we can better understand their population and the potential threats to their survival.

FANGTOOTH MORAY

Enchelycore anatina

(en-chel-eye-core a-na-tee-na)

The fangtooth moray's creepiest feature is its icicle-like teeth, which grow up to 1 inch (2.5 cm) long and fill the eel's large mouth in two rows. The largest teeth are in the first row, and the second row contains smaller teeth.

Those teeth can cause a nasty bite! You may come across a few tales of people being bitten by fangtooth morays, but it's not common. Despite their intimidating appearance, these eels are typically timid and peaceful, unless they feel extremely scared or threatened.

Their snake-like bodies can reach up to 4 feet (120 cm) long, and a long dorsal fin runs down the length of their back, allowing them to swim smoothly and quickly through the water, either to escape a threat or to chase their dinner.

Where They Live

These eels are quite difficult to find—they hide in rocky crevasses, corals, and caves at depths of 35 to 165 feet (10–50 m) for most of their lives. They're most likely to live in the Atlantic Ocean—around the Canary Islands, Bermuda, and Brazil, for instance—but they can also be found in the Mediterranean Sea.

What They Eat

Their long, sharp teeth help them to bite and eat crustaceans, which make up the majority of their diet. Since they have poor eyesight and mainly hunt at night, morays rely heavily on their sense of smell to find prey. They like to remain tucked inside their hideaways, emerging only to pounce on the small fish and crustaceans who swim by.

Conservation Status

LEAST CONCERN

This species of moray eel is one of the lucky ones—it has no known threats and is rarely impacted by humans. There could be a few reasons for this. Because they stay hidden for most of their lives, they may not come across many threats. They may also intimidate other animals and occupy a spot at the top of their food chain. Their menacing appearance certainly frightens humans whenever we come across them in the wild!

FUN FACTS

✳ Do these eels look like tigers to you? Sometimes they're called tiger morays because of their black and yellow stripes.

✳ Fangtooth morays often open and close their mouths, showing off their many teeth. This isn't meant to be frightening, though—they're actually pumping fresh water through their gills, which helps them breathe.

✳ The fangtooth moray has a symbiotic relationship with the white striped cleaner shrimp, which means these two species help each other out. Like very tiny dentists, these shrimp venture into the eel's mouth to clean parasites and food scraps off its teeth—and even though the moray finds crustaceans scrumptious, it won't eat the shrimp! Everyone benefits from this relationship: The shrimp gets to eat dinner, and the eel gets clean teeth.

✳ This eel's range may be expanding—recently, one was found living in the Aegean Sea between Greece and Turkey.

GELADA BABOON

Theropithecus gelada

(thero-pith-e-kus gell-ada)

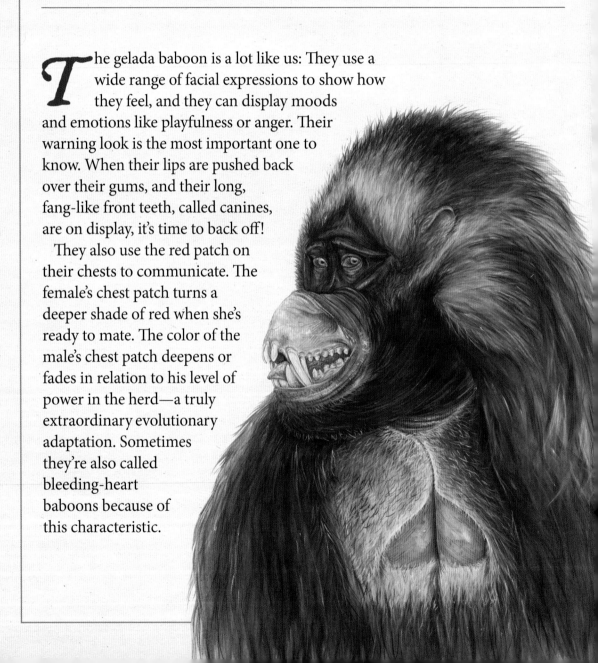

The gelada baboon is a lot like us: They use a wide range of facial expressions to show how they feel, and they can display moods and emotions like playfulness or anger. Their warning look is the most important one to know. When their lips are pushed back over their gums, and their long, fang-like front teeth, called canines, are on display, it's time to back off!

They also use the red patch on their chests to communicate. The female's chest patch turns a deeper shade of red when she's ready to mate. The color of the male's chest patch deepens or fades in relation to his level of power in the herd—a truly extraordinary evolutionary adaptation. Sometimes they're also called bleeding-heart baboons because of this characteristic.

Although both sexes have brown fur, males grow a magnificent mane and are usually larger than the females. They average around 4 feet (125 cm) tall and weigh around 45 pounds (20.5 kg), about 11 pounds (5 kg) heavier than females.

Where They Live

To see these monkeys in their natural habitats, you'll have to travel to the highlands of Ethiopia and Eritrea. You'll also need to climb steep cliffs and rocky gorges, where they like to huddle together at night. Even though they like to sleep in the cliffs, geladas are primarily terrestrial, meaning they spend most of their lives on the ground.

What They Eat

You may think they're hunters and meat eaters because of their gigantic, terrifying teeth, but geladas are more or less vegetarian, and actually eat grass most of the time! They use their human-like hands to pick the most delicious blades of grass and avoid the less tasty ones. In drier months, when the grasses they love aren't available, they're forced to feed on roots, flowers, fruit, and the occasional insect instead.

Conservation Status

LEAST CONCERN

Although the gelada's habitat is being destroyed by humans to clear land for livestock and crops, these monkeys are not considered at risk. The species has some protections, but people are still allowed to hunt and kill them, whether for food or trophies or because they're seen as a nuisance to farmers.

GIANT ANTEATER

Myrmecophaga tridactyla

(murm-e-cof-aga tri-dak-til-a)

Giant anteaters have no teeth, but they do have incredibly long snouts and fast-moving tongues. Measuring 6.5 feet (2 m) from head to tail and weighing up to 145 pounds (65 kg), these insect-eaters have long, sharp claws, which they use to eat their favorite foods: ants and termites. First, they slash holes in an ant or termite mound. Then they shove their tubular noses into the hole and use their 2-foot-long (60 cm) tongues to collect up to 35,000 ants and termites a day! How do they do this? Their tongues are covered with sticky saliva and tiny, backward-facing barbs that trap the insects.

They also have a large bushy tail that can make it hard to tell which end is which! Their tail also comes in handy as a blanket in the colder months and a source of shade in the hotter months.

Where They Live

Sadly, giant anteaters are now extinct in Guatemala and Belize, but they can still be found in other parts of Central and South America, such as Argentina, Paraguay, and Bolivia. They enjoy a variety of habitats, but are usually found in grasslands, forests, and plantations.

What They Eat

Since they have to eat such an enormous quantity of ants and termites every day just to survive, giant anteaters have developed the ability to move their tongues as fast as 160 times a minute! (But that's the only thing about them that moves quickly—like their relatives the sloths, they conserve their energy by keeping their other movements slow.) Amazingly, giant anteaters aren't immune to ant bites! That's part of why they have to eat so quickly— they spend only a minute or so slurping up ants at each mound.

Close Relations

Anteaters, armadillos, and sloths are all part of a group of mammals called Xenarthra. These mammals have certain key features in common—for example, they all have razor-sharp claws.

Conservation Status

VULNERABLE

The anteater has survived for 25 million years on earth, yet in the past 10 years, it's started to disappear at a rapid rate because of land loss, poaching, and car accidents. In places like Brazil, people catch and kill the giant anteater for its supposed medicinal uses, as well as for food and leather products. Unfortunately, there may be only about 5,000 left in the wild.

FUN FACTS

* Baby anteaters ride on their mother's back, which makes the mother look larger and more threatening.

* Despite their prehistoric appearance, giant anteaters live only as long as a typical dog— around 14 years.

* Their claws can also be used in self-defense and to protect their young against predators. They've even been known to kill jaguars!

GOBLIN SHARK

Mitsukurina owstoni

(mit-soo-kur-e-na o-stone-e)

The goblin shark is a secretive beast. These sharks spend most of their time deep in the ocean and are very rarely seen by other animals—even by other goblin sharks. They're definitely not the loveliest specimens, but there's a good reason for their gruesome appearance.

Unlike other sharks, the goblin shark has retractable, flexible jaws, which means they can very quickly thrust their mouth outward, crammed full of menacing teeth, to snap up passing meals. This helps them catch prey without having to propel their whole body forward. Such a large deep-sea animal needs to conserve energy as much as possible, so this adaptation is very useful.

Goblin sharks grow to around 13 feet (4 m) long. Except for their pinkish-purple coloring, they resemble most other species of shark when their jaws aren't extended.

Where They Live

Scientists believe goblin sharks live mainly in the waters around Japan, because that's where the most recorded sightings have taken place. However, they've also been spotted throughout the Atlantic, Pacific, and Indian Oceans, and even off the coasts of New South Wales and Tasmania in Australia. To find them yourself, you must be at depths of 130 to 4,265 feet (40–1,300 m), hanging out near the seabed.

What They Eat

With their powerful mouths, they feast on squid, fish, crabs, and crustaceans. Because there's so little light deep in the ocean, goblin sharks, like other deep-sea creatures, don't really need good eyesight. Instead, they rely on their snout—not to sniff out their prey, but to find it with electricity! Their snout is full of electroreceptors: special sensory cells that allow them to pick up electrical signals. This allows them to burrow through the seabed and sense where potential prey may be hiding.

Conservation Status

LEAST CONCERN

Little is known about these deep-water sharks. However, researchers believe there are very few threats to their survival other than being accidentally caught by deep-sea trawlers, which also harm their seafloor habitats.

FUN FACTS

✳ Goblin shark jaws and teeth are highly sought after and can be sold for up to $5,000 apiece.

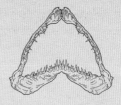

✳ Humans have been unable to study these sharks in their natural habitat because they live in such deep waters.

✳ Fewer than 50 specimens have been found in the past 118 years.

✳ Say aah! Human jaws can open about 50 degrees. The goblin shark's jaw can open 110 degrees, more than twice as wide as ours!

✳ When fully extended, their jaws can measure more than 9 percent of their total body length.

GREATER SAGE GROUSE

Centrocercus urophasianus

(cent-ro-ser-cus yu-ro-fas-e-a-nus)

It's easy to tell the difference between the male and female sage grouse. That's because the male boasts some of the most unusual avian accessories around: two large, yellow, egg-shaped air sacs, which he can inflate with about a gallon of air just by breathing in. They're quite a sight! When filled, the male can shake them to make wobbly, popping noises. Why? To attract a mate during breeding season, of course. The male sage grouse will also show off by fanning his magnificent tail feathers. In comparison, the females, with their grey-brown plumage, appear quite plain!

Greater sage grouse can reach up to 2 feet (60 cm) tall and weigh up to around 6.5 pounds (3 kg).

Where They Live

As their name suggests, the sage grouse lives in sagebrush plains. They are North American birds, native to the western United States and southeastern Canada. Between March and May, sage grouse will visit their courting grounds, known as leks, to complete their mating displays.

What They Eat

These birds mainly eat plants and will spend their days dining on fresh shoots and leaves. In warmer months, they'll also eat small insects and flowers. Ideally, their habitat will have a water source close by, but if this isn't possible, sage grouse will fly up to 3 miles (5 km) twice a day for a drink.

Conservation Status

NEAR THREATENED

Due to the ever-increasing demand for crops such as wheat and potatoes, as well as products like oil and gas, the sage grouse's habitat is quickly being lost, which has caused their population to decline. Sage grouse are very sensitive to human disruption, and their numbers provide a good indication of how healthy the ecosystem is. Unfortunately, humans now use so many of the areas where the sage grouse used to live that the birds inhabit only half of their original range.

FUN FACTS

* The typical life span of a sage grouse is three to six years. Females often outlive males, though, because people hunt the males for their stunning feathers.

* In the winter, the sage grouse gets water by eating snow.

* As many as 70 males (or more!) can be present during mating displays, generally only one or two of them will be chosen as mates by the females.

HAIRLESS CHINESE CRESTED DOG

Canis lupus familiaris

(kay-nis loo-pus fam-ili-aris)

FRANKIE

The Chinese crested dog comes in two different varieties: the hairless and the powderpuff. Of the two, the hairless has the more unfortunate features, with tufts of hair growing only on parts of its face, feet, and tail. Plus, hairless dog breeds tend to have poor teeth, so the hairless Chinese crested dog often has an odd, gappy-toothed look.

These dogs are about the size of a house cat, weighing only 10 pounds (4.5 kg) and growing to a mere 13 inches (33 cm) long.

Where They Live

This breed of dog became common as a house pet in North America around 1974. But they didn't actually originate in China, as their name would have you believe. They were actually bred from Mexican and African hairless dogs, and can now be found all over the world. Since these dogs are so small, they don't need a lot of exercise and are well suited to live in small houses or apartments.

What They Eat

Like most domesticated dogs, this breed subsists on a range of prepackaged dog foods, rather than going out and hunting for themselves!

Conservation Status

NOT EVALUATED

The Chinese crested dog is a domesticated dog, so its conservation status has never been evaluated. However, records going as far back as the late 1800s suggest they are abundant, and have been for a long time.

FUN FACTS

* Hairless Chinese crested dogs will live for approximately 12 years.

* Because they don't have hair on most of their body, they can struggle with skin conditions. They're even prone to getting blackheads!

* In the 1500s, the ancestors of Chinese crested dogs may have been used on ships to help rid the vessels of rats and mice, which were potential carriers of the plague.

* Their Mexican ancestors were also used by Aztecs as portable sources of heat in colder climates.

* They're one of the most popular breeds to enter the World's Ugliest Dog Contest, and they often take home the prize!

HAMMER-HEADED FRUIT BAT

Hypsignathus monstrosus
(hip-sig-nay-thus mon-stro-sus)

The male hammer-headed fruit bat has a shockingly large nose and giant, drooping lips that make it look a little like a moose. Why such an enormous snout? To produce loud honking sounds that attract female bats! The sexes vary significantly in size and weight, with the females averaging 8 inches (20 cm) and 10 ounces (280 g), and males averaging 10 inches (25 cm) and 13 ounces (370 g). An adult bat's wingspan can be nearly 3 feet (1 m) wide.

Where They Live

You can find hammer-headed fruit bats in mangrove swamps, rivers, and palm forests along the equator in West and Central Africa. They like to perch in trees in small groups of around five bats.

What They Eat

Figs, guavas, bananas, and mangoes make up most of the hammer-headed fruit bat's diet, and males have been known to travel up to 6 miles (10 km) in search of the best fruit. They're called fruit bats for a reason!

Close Relations

The hammer-headed fruit bat is closely related to the bat family Pteropodidae, sometimes called the Old World fruit bats.

Conservation Status

LEAST CONCERN

Humans occasionally hunt and eat this species, but its most immediate threat is the destruction of its habitat for logging. These bats can also be infected by deadly parasites.

HELLBENDER

Cryptobranchus alleganiensis

(crip-toe-brank-us al-eg-a-ni-en-sis)

Hellbenders have existed for 160 million years, which explains their prehistoric appearance! Females can reach lengths of 30 inches (75 cm) and males can measure 27 inches (68.5 cm), making them the third-largest salamander on earth and the largest in North America. Most are around 8 to 12 inches (20–30 cm) shorter than this, though. They weigh anywhere between 14 and 36 ounces (400–1,010 g).

These salamanders secrete a form of mucus or goo from their skin that makes them extremely slimy. This helps them move smoothly over rocky or muddy terrain and also protects them from predators—the slime tastes terrible, and anything that tries to bite a hellbender will quickly change its mind! It's also the origin of their somewhat unfortunate nickname: "snot otters."

Where They Live

The hellbender is a freshwater aquatic amphibian that you'll find living 6 to 24 inches (15–60 cm) below the surface of swift-running streams, rivers, and creeks throughout the eastern United States. They can be tricky to see because they like to rest during the day and hunt at night, and because they like to hide beneath large sticks and logs in rocky, muddy areas.

What They Eat

They mainly dine on crayfish and the occasional fish, insect, tadpole, or smaller salamander. By studying captured specimens whose stomachs had mud and rocks in them, scientists have learned that hellbenders are bottom feeders. Curiously, these salamanders sometimes snack on their own eggs during mating season. Fortunately, they don't eat all of them! They leave most to grow and hatch.

Conservation Status

NEAR THREATENED

Hellbenders face a number of serious threats, including pollution and habitat loss. Their homes and nesting sites are found at the base of rocky environments, where they can be easily impacted or destroyed by human activities like mining and logging. Human superstition also puts the hellbender at risk—many fishermen believe they are deadly and will kill them on sight. Plus, their popularity as pets and in the collection trade means their numbers in the wild are dwindling.

FUN FACTS

* Hellbenders can live to be 30 years old, but they usually reach only half that age due to over-capturing, pollution, and habitat destruction.

* They can lay up to 450 eggs in just one month out of a year, usually September to October.

* No one knows exactly how they got their name. It may have come from fishermen who described them as looking "like they crawled out of hell and are bent on going back."

* They breathe entirely through their skin, which is why they need to live in clean, clear water.

* Hellbenders have been known to swallow fish nearly as large as they are!

HELMETED GUINEAFOWL

Numida meleagris

(nu-me-da mel-e-a-gris)

Although the helmeted guineafowl's feathers are generally thought to be quite beautiful, their wrinkly, featherless heads are considerably less so. Like the southern cassowary (page 108), these birds have dangling wattles that are more vibrant in the males, probably to attract a mate. They also have a horn that's a little like the cassowary's, although no one knows what the helmeted guineafowl uses it for.

They are very vocal birds, whether trying to win a mate or when they're feeling threatened. Many farmers who own these guineafowl find they make great replacements for guard dogs, as they raise an alarm if animals or humans try to intrude. They're about the size of a small chicken.

Where They Live

In the wild, these guineafowl live in a variety of habitats such as bush, forests, grasslands, or even deserts now and then. They've also adapted to living in suburban neighborhoods outside cities in South Africa, where they roam the streets in flocks. They are native to many regions of Africa, but their growing popularity as pets and farm animals means they can now be found all over the world, including Australia and the United States.

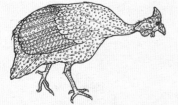

What They Eat

Whether out of curiosity or hunger, helmeted guineafowl love to eat creatures that humans consider pests, like small snakes, ticks, and rodents. This is part of why they're so popular as pets! They also eat seeds, berries, and plants.

Conservation Status

LEAST CONCERN

The helmeted guineafowl's numbers are stable because the birds are farmed for their eggs, meat, and feathers, and because they're kept as pets. Their skittish nature and small size make them attractive to many predators, though, such as wild dogs, cats, and large snakes.

HELMETED HORNBILL

Rhinoplax vigil

(ry-no-plax vig-il)

These giant, eye-catching birds are one of the largest species of hornbill and can reach 4 feet (120 cm) tall—and that doesn't include their tail feathers. Those feathers can measure up to 1.5 feet (50 cm) long on their own!

Their horns are around 1 foot (30 cm) long on average and weigh in at around 6.5 pounds (3 kg) for males and 6 pounds (2.5 kg) for females—that's 10 percent of the birds' total body weight.

Helmeted hornbills use these horns, also known as casques, to defend their mates, eggs, and territory from other hornbills. This species is sexually dimorphic: The females have a pale blue wrinkled neck pouch, whereas the males' neck pouch is deep burgundy.

Where They Live

Native to the Southeast Asian countries of Indonesia, Malaysia, Thailand, Borneo, Myanmar, Sumatra, and Brunei, these birds live high up in the trees of lowland, semievergreen, or evergreen forests. The trees they prefer will have high branches for the males to keep watch from, and suitable nesting nooks for the females.

What They Eat

Despite their fierce-looking beaks, these hornbills feast mainly on fruit. They're excellent seed dispersers—they don't digest the seeds from the fruit they eat, instead distributing them around the forest through their droppings. They've also been spotted eating small animals, like snakes and insects, and even large birds, including their fellow hornbills!

Conservation Status

CRITICALLY ENDANGERED

Unfortunately, this irreplaceable species may become extinct in the near future. Large portions of their habitat have been cleared for logging and palm oil plantations, and they are hunted for their unique horns, which are made of a material people call "red ivory." Their casques are used to make jewelry and ornaments and can be sold for large sums of money.

In 2013, as many as 6,000 hornbills were killed for trade purposes in West Kalimantan in Borneo. Although hunting the helmeted hornbill has been illegal for years, and is punishable by up to five years in prison, these amazing birds are still killed and traded. To save this species from extinction, people must enforce these laws and initiate projects to help the birds recover.

FUN FACTS

✳ There are 60 species of hornbill, but this is the only one with a solid casque. The casque is made entirely of keratin and is fused to the bird's skull.

✳ The Bornean Dayak tribe believes these birds are messengers from the gods, and so killing them is forbidden.

✳ Mating couples seal their nesting hollows with their own poo to protect the female and her babies.

✳ When they fight, helmeted hornbills sometimes fly directly into one another and crash heads, creating a sound that can be heard over 325 feet (100 m) away.

✳ If they eat too many fermented figs, they can get tipsy!

HUMPBACK ANGLERFISH

Melanocetus johnsonii

(mel-on-o-see-tus john-so-nee-eye)

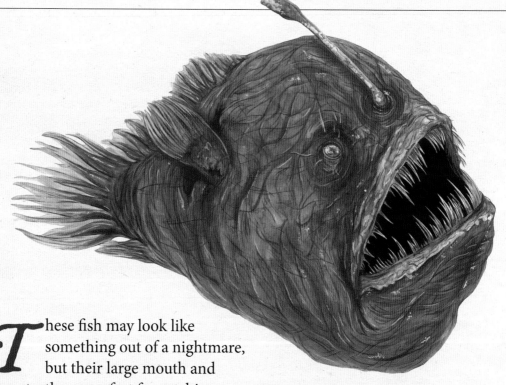

These fish may look like something out of a nightmare, but their large mouth and long teeth are perfect for catching a meal in the deep sea.

Humpback anglerfish live so deep in the ocean that no sunlight can reach them—so they've got their own source of light, known as an esca or illicium. This organ extends from their forehead and lures passing prey, drawing them in close enough for the anglerfish to devour. The light comes from bacteria that glow, a phenomenon known as bioluminescence. Only females have an esca, though, and they also use it to attract a mate.

The females of this species are approximately five times larger than the males and are also more dominant. Females can reach up to 6 inches (15.5 cm) long, whereas males only grow to 1 inch (3 cm)—a case of extreme sexual dimorphism!

Where They Live

The humpback anglerfish lives in the Indian, Atlantic, and Pacific Oceans. However, you won't be able to meet one of these fish in person, as they live deep down in the ocean—up to 6,890 feet (2,100 m) deep!—in cold, dark regions called the mesopelagic and bathypelagic zones.

What They Eat

Because of their esca, or lure, these fish don't need to be speedy swimmers, which explains why their bodies are so round.

Instead, they drift slowly through the water, waiting for prey to come to them. They eat animals such as other fish, jellyfish, and krill, and can use their sharp, angled teeth and large mouths to capture and eat prey twice their size.

Conservation Status

LEAST CONCERN

Despite living so far away from people, humpback anglerfish still face threats caused by humans. They can be accidentally caught in trawlers, and the health of their deep-sea home can be negatively affected by climate change.

FUN FACTS

* These anglerfish are also called humpback blackdevils.

* Only 8 male specimens have ever been found, in contrast to 852 females!

* In other anglerfish, the male latches on to the female's body after mating and becomes parasitic, sharing her blood supply. Luckily, this isn't the case for this species.

* These fish have very tiny eyes in proportion to their bodies—since they live in total darkness, they don't need to see that well!

* The males have only one purpose in life: search for a mate, latch on, fertilize the egg, then take off to find another female.

KING VULTURE

Sarcoramphus papa

(sark-o-ram-fus pa-pa)

With their vivid yellow, orange, and red heads and their dramatic white and black feathers, king vultures are the most colorful of their kind. They don't have eyelashes, like other vultures do, but they do have a stunning red ring around each eye.

These vultures are gigantic birds! Their wingspan can measure almost 6.5 feet (2 m) and they can grow to 2.5 feet (80 cm) from head to tail. They usually weigh up to 10 pounds (4.5 kg).

The king vulture is a sexually monomorphic bird, which means both sexes look the same. Like other vultures, they're bald, a trait that evolved to prevent them from getting diseases after feasting on dead animals.

Where They Live

King vultures live in Argentina, Mexico, and other regions of Central and South America. They don't migrate, but stay in the same area all year round. Spotting them is rather difficult because they make their homes in the highest treetops. They prefer forested environments and lay their eggs in logs and hollow stumps rather than building nests.

What They Eat

These birds are scavengers, meaning they don't kill their food themselves but instead eat roadkill, leftovers from other predators, or animals that have died of natural causes like sickness or old age. This way of eating may not sound appetizing to us, but it's extremely beneficial for the environment, as it cleans up decaying carcasses, which helps prevent the spread of pathogens.

Close Relations

King vultures are closely related to the turkey vulture (page 118).

Conservation Status

LEAST CONCERN

With around 50,000 individual king vultures alive today, they're not considered to be endangered. But their habitats are being destroyed by logging and deforestation, so their numbers are currently declining. More immediate threats include snakes that prey on their eggs and large mammals that attack them when they're vulnerable.

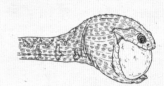

FUN FACTS

※ King vultures can live for up to 30 years!

※ Paradoxically, the term for a group of king vultures is a solitary.

※ They make their nesting sites extra stinky by regurgitating food in and around them. Scientists believe they do this to discourage predators.

※ They're at their most vulnerable after meals, because they can't take flight easily with a stomach full of food. If they need to, they'll vomit up their dinner to make themselves light enough for takeoff!

※ Their name may come from a Mayan legend in which this species was a king who transferred messages between the gods and humans.

※ The fleshy growths on their beaks are called caruncles, and are similar to the wattles on turkeys and chickens.

LARGETOOTH SAWFISH

Pristis pristis
(pris-tis pris-tis)

Largetooth sawfish get their name from the sharp growths along both sides of their long rostrum, or snout—these look like teeth, but are actually scales! Like the goblin shark and the Australian ghost shark (pages 50 and 20), the sawfish uses electroreceptors to locate their prey in muddy riverbeds. Then they stun and dismember their dinner with their spiny, chainsaw-like rostrum.

Their mouths are on their undersides, in the perfect position to suction up fast-moving prey beneath them. They can grow to massive lengths of over 21 feet (6.5 m) from tip to tail, and can weigh as much as 1,320 pounds (600 kg)!

Where They Live

Largetooth sawfish have been found living in the waters around Southeast Asia and New Guinea and in the western Indian Ocean. Large numbers of them live off the coast of northern Australia as well, where there are measures in place to protect them and help keep their numbers up. Since their body is long and flat, they like to lay low on muddy riverbeds, where they're easily camouflaged. Sawfish live in freshwater environments such as rivers and estuaries and prefer to hang out at depths of around 33 feet (10 m).

What They Eat

With such a long, intimidating snout, you'd expect largetooth sawfish to be a vicious threat to most sea creatures, but they don't mess with bigger fish, preferring to fill up on small invertebrates, schools of fish, and crustaceans.

Conservation Status

CRITICALLY ENDANGERED

No one knows how many largetooth sawfish there actually are—they aren't seen very often, and they're often confused for other fish. But many scientists think they've already become extinct in many of the places they once lived. They tend to get caught in fishing nets accidentally and are also hunted for their body parts—people covet their unique snouts and their skin, which is turned into leather and made into clothing.

Around 1,000 to 2,000 sawfish snouts are sold in Brazil's fish markets every year. People use the tooth-like scales on their rostrums to decorate weapons and to make soup!

FUN FACTS

* Although they prefer freshwater habitats, largetooth sawfish are euryhaline, which means they can survive in saltwater, too.

* The oldest recorded largetooth sawfish was estimated to be 35 years old.

* Baby sawfish don't hatch from an egg laid on the riverbed like many other underwater species. Instead, sawfish eggs are incubated inside their mother until the young are ready to emerge and swim on their own.

* Sawfish look a lot like sharks, but they're actually rays, which tend to be flatter than sharks.

MALAYAN TAPIR

Tapirus indicus

(tay-peer-us in-deek-us)

It may look incredibly strange, but the Malayan tapir's thick, trunk-like nose is a truly handy adaptation. Perfect for plucking leaves off trees, it also acts as a built-in snorkel when a tapir takes a swim.

The tapir's black-and-white colors also serve a purpose. These animals are mainly nocturnal (they're most active at night), and this coloration helps them blend in with the tree trunks as they roam through the forest looking for food.

The Malayan tapir is the largest species of tapir in the world, weighing an average of 605 pounds (275 kg)—but they can weigh as much as 1,190 pounds (540 kg) and grow to lengths of 8 feet (2.5 m)!

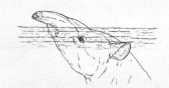

Where They Live

They're native to parts of Malaysia, Indonesia, Thailand, and Myanmar, and since they love to wallow in pools of water to cool down, they can be found in lowland habitats. They move to hilly forests for the rainy seasons. Tapirs usually live alone, though mothers and their young will live together for up to eight months.

What They Eat

The Malayan tapir dines on grass and the leaves, fruits, and flowers of small trees.

Close Relations

Its nose looks a little like an elephant's trunk, but the tapir's closest relatives are actually the common horse and the rhinoceros. Both rhinos and tapirs have three toes on their back feet!

Conservation Status

ENDANGERED

Tapirs are seriously threatened by habitat loss as people clear land to make room for palm oil plantations and other industries. Plus, as deforestation causes other species to die out, tapirs are being targeted by new predators who can't find enough of their usual prey. Humans also hunt tapirs, even though it's illegal.

FUN FACTS

* A group of tapirs is called a candle.

* The Malayan tapir has the longest snout of all the tapir species.

* To mark their territory, they like to spray their urine over long distances. So if you ever find yourself near a tapir, make sure to stand far away!

* Tapirs love to poo in the water.

MALEO

Macrocephalon maleo

(ma-cro-sef-a-lon mal-e-o)

Do you see that bump on the maleo's head? It's a bony horn called a casque, like the ones atop the heads of the helmeted hornbill and the southern cassowary (pages 62 and 108). But why the maleo has a casque, no one knows! Both males and females have one, so it probably doesn't play a role in attracting a mate.

Standing at around 2 feet (60 cm) tall, with whitish-pink feathers on their bellies, these shy birds don't usually make a sound unless they're near their nesting grounds or they feel threatened. They take turns standing guard over their nests and watching for predators.

Where They Live

The maleo is native, or endemic, to two regions of Indonesia: Buton Island and Sulawesi. They like to nest in groups—with more birds around, they're better protected against predators. Maleos nest in riverbanks and sandy floors, digging pits in the ground with their large feet and laying their gigantic eggs before covering them with sand. The birds rely on heat from the sun to keep the nest warm for two to three months. If the temperature of the sand drops or rises too drastically, the chicks won't survive.

What They Eat

Like other birds from this part of Indonesia, maleos spend their days feeding on a range of seeds, roots, and fruits, as well as small invertebrates such as insects.

Conservation Status

ENDANGERED

Maleo eggs are considered a delicacy these days, and so people in Indonesia collect and sell them for money. The bird's habitat is also being destroyed by deforestation and commercial logging. Invasive species like dogs and rats have been introduced to the area, and they hunt the maleo and their chicks. In the past 50 years, the population of maleos has declined by 90 percent.

FUN FACTS

✳ When maleos reach adolescence, they find the partner they will stay with for life.

✳ Maleo eggs are enormous in comparison to their bodies, and can be around five times the size of a chicken egg!

✳ Because their eggs are so big, female maleos will often faint from exhaustion while laying them.

✳ Their chicks hatch underground, and it can take the baby maleos up to two days to dig to the surface and begin their lives.

MANDRILL

Mandrillus sphinx

(man-drill-us sfinks)

It's impossible to ignore the brilliant colors that adorn the mandrill's face and rump. These colors aren't there just to make them look good—they actually help these primates communicate with each other. For instance, patches of red and blue skin on their rump, chest, wrists, and ankles will grow brighter to signify excitement or submissiveness, or to show that they're ready to mate.

They also express their emotions by opening their mouths, which lets other mandrills know they're happy and feeling friendly. When they open their mouths even wider, showing off their 2-inch-long (4.5 cm) teeth in a gesture known as "yawning," they're letting potential threats know they're angry.

Males and females of this species don't look exactly the same. Males can grow up to 3 feet (90 cm) tall and weigh 110 pounds (50 kg), whereas the females are significantly smaller, about half the size of the males. Females are also much less colorful.

Where They Live

Mandrills are terrestrial, meaning they spend most of their time on the ground. They live in the forests and thick scrub of central west Africa, in areas around the Congo River, western Gabon, and Equatorial Guinea. To keep themselves safe from predators, mandrills will climb into trees to sleep at night. A group of these primates can be as large as fifty individuals. Usually, there's only one male per group. His role is to protect the group from danger and mate with the females.

What They Eat

Mandrills eat all sorts of plants, insects, and small animals—roots, flowers, leaves, snails, worms, snakes, lizards, and more.

Conservation Status

VULNERABLE

People in Africa hunt mandrills for their prized meat, and the monkey's loud, distinctive calls make them easy to track down. Because of this, as well as the destruction of their habitat through logging and deforestation, mandrills have lost over 30 percent of their population since the 1990s. Humans must now protect these incredible primates to keep them from going extinct.

FUN FACTS

* When mandrills are angry, they'll ferociously hit the ground.

* Females in a group will help to raise babies that are not their own.

* They've been known to live as long as 46 years.

* Like humans, these primates have opposable thumbs, which they use to grip branches and climb trees.

* A group of mandrills is called a barrel or a wilderness.

MARABOU STORK

Leptoptilos crumenifer

(lep-top-til-os crew-men-i-fer)

Nicknamed the "undertaker bird" because of their plumage, which makes them look like they're wearing a black suit with coattails, these bald, gangly birds can reach 5 feet (1.5 m) tall, with a wingspan of 8.5 feet (2.5 m) when they're fully grown.

Beneath their gigantic beaks—which can grow up to 10 inches (25 cm) long—the male storks sport a large, fleshy, pink pouch that's connected to their nostrils. During mating displays, they entice females by inflating this pouch and making a croaking sound. Marabou storks mate for life, and both the male and female bird help feed and protect their young.

Where They Live

Native to Africa, south of the Sahara Desert, these unique birds dwell in open areas near water, such as riverbanks and swamps. Sometimes they live close to humans, near garbage dumps, stockyards, or fishing villages. Marabou storks build their nests out of sticks and twigs, way up high in the treetops.

What They Eat

Marabou storks are scavengers, meaning they eat animals that are already dead. They play an important role in the ecosystem by cleaning up decaying leftovers from water sources and preventing the spread of disease. However, they will kill other animals to eat, such as small mammals, birds, and insects. They're especially drawn to grass fires, where they'll snap up fleeing creatures in their beaks for dinner.

Conservation Status

LEAST CONCERN

The marabou stork's ugly appearance doesn't protect it from being hunted and sold at markets across Africa for its feathers and meat. Nevertheless, their population continues to grow as the number of landfills increases, providing this resilient scavenger with an endless supply of food.

FUN FACTS

* African folklore says that God made the marabou stork out of leftover parts from other animals, which is why it's such a homely bird.

* Marabou storks have hollow legs and toes so they'll be light enough to fly.

* They can live to the ripe old age of 25 in the wild.

* They deliberately poo on themselves and let the poo run down their legs! It decontaminates their legs and cools them down.

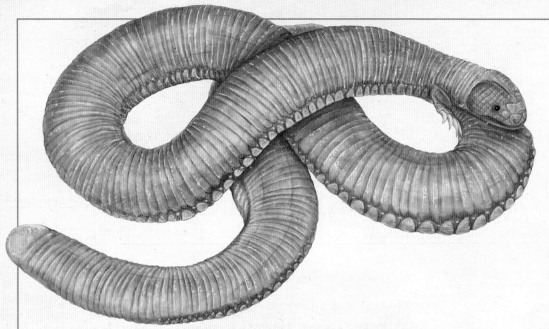

MEXICAN MOLE LIZARD

Bipes biporus
(bye-pees bye-poor-us)

There's no way to tell a female Mexican mole lizard from a male—both sexes are pinkish in color and look like overgrown earthworms with tiny front limbs. However, you can distinguish between young lizards and adults. As they grow older, these lizards not only grow longer—up to 7 inches (19 cm)—but also fade to a paler shade of pink. And older lizards are more likely to be missing their tails! Amazingly, they're able to detach their own tail when chased by a predator, leaving it behind to distract the hunter while the lizard flees.

The mole lizard's body, front limbs, and claws are well adapted to traveling and digging through tight burrows. It can even adjust its body temperature according to the surrounding soil.

Where They Live

It's tricky to spot these animals in their natural habitat, as they spend most of their time underground in the tunnel systems they build, avoiding almost all threats and predators. If you do want to go searching, you'll need to start by traveling to the Baja California Peninsula on the west coast of Mexico.

What They Eat

The Mexican mole lizard eats an enormous amount of mites, ants, termites, cockroaches, and other small insects and animals, which makes them a fantastic form of pest control for neighboring humans. Despite their small size, they'll attempt to eat almost any creature that will fit into their mouths.

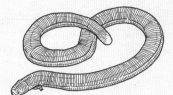

Conservation Status

LEAST CONCERN

Local people sometimes mistake the weird-looking mole lizard for a snake and kill it. However, this unusual reptile poses no threat to humans and is as harmless as a large earthworm. Its habitat isn't under threat and its numbers are stable, so the Mexican mole lizard is considered safe from extinction, at least for the time being.

FUN FACTS

❋ Mexican mole lizards can't regrow their tail, so they have to use their detachment strategy wisely.

❋ These reptiles aren't lizards or snakes. Instead, they're part of a group called amphisbaenians. Out of the 200 animals in this group, there are only 3 that have limbs, and the Mexican mole lizard is one of them.

❋ Mexican mole lizards don't live very long—the oldest one on record was three years old.

❋ Aside from their human predators, they're sometimes killed by mammals such as skunks, who come across the lizards while digging in the dirt.

MONKEY SLUG CATERPILLAR

Phobetron pithecium

(fobe-tron pith-e-see-um)

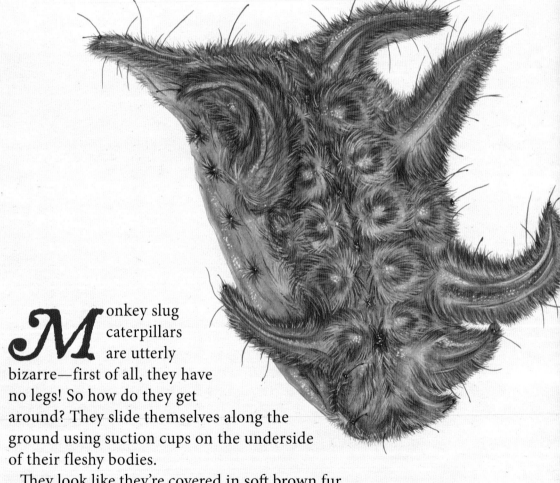

Monkey slug caterpillars are utterly bizarre—first of all, they have no legs! So how do they get around? They slide themselves along the ground using suction cups on the underside of their fleshy bodies.

They look like they're covered in soft brown fur, but these are actually tiny, sharp hairs that will sting anything that touches them. And in case that wasn't strange enough, they have six leg-like "limbs" growing out of their furry upper bodies. These aren't actual legs, but they make the caterpillar look bigger and more menacing than it actually is.

Monkey slugs can be up to 1 inch (2.5 cm) long.

Where They Live

These caterpillars, and the moths they turn into, live in eastern Canada and the United States, from Quebec to Arkansas and everywhere in between—wherever their favorite trees grow. These include willows, apples, chestnuts, oaks, and many others.

What They Eat

Scientists don't know much about the diet of the monkey slug caterpillar, but it probably eats the leaves of bushes and trees such as oaks.

Once monkey slugs have transformed into moths, they slurp up sap, fruit juice, and flower nectar through their straw-like tongue, otherwise known as a proboscis.

Conservation Status

NOT EVALUATED

Like *Creatonotos gangis*, monkey slug caterpillars are something of a mystery. We don't know much about them, and their conservation status hasn't been evaluated. Hopefully, more research will be done in the future so we can understand their population and the threats they may face.

FUN FACTS

* The monkey slug caterpillar turns into the hag moth, which is also very furry, but at least has proper legs!

* Their intimidating appearance seems to deter small predators. Only a monkey slug is brave enough to take on another monkey slug.

* Males and females look the same, which is known as monomorphism.

* When they create their cocoon, monkey slugs place their hairy limb-like growths on the outside of it to ward off predators.

* Because of their suction cups, they can't move very fast. Even a regular slug might be able to outrun (or out-slide!) a monkey slug.

NAKED MOLE RAT

Heterocephalus glaber

(het-e-ro-sef-a-lus gla-ber)

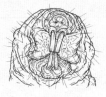

*T*hese remarkable rats don't have a coat of soft fur, just a few whiskers here and there. You'd think they'd get cold being naked all the time, but they stay warm in their underground homes by huddling next to other mole rats. They also don't feel pain the same way we do, and wouldn't be bothered if they were dipped into a bowl of acid or hot sauce. (Ouch!)

That's not all—they live in burrows that they dig with their teeth, which are on the outside of their mouths.

This allows them to dig without swallowing dirt. They're also able to move these teeth independently of each other, like a pair of chopsticks! They have very loose skin that helps them pass each other easily in narrow underground tunnels without getting stuck.

Finally, they're the only mammal that lives in a colony with one queen and many workers, like ants do.

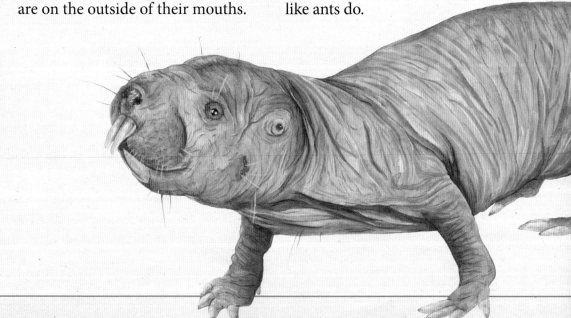

Worker rats average up to 3 inches (7.5 cm) long and weigh around 1 ounce (30 g). The queen rat runs the colony and gives birth to new young, and she can weigh as much as 2.5 ounces (70 g).

Where They Live

These wrinkly rats build their burrows in areas of eastern Africa like central Ethiopia, Somalia, Kenya, and Djibouti, but you'll never see them outside of a zoo—unless you happen to live underground too! They live in intricate networks of tunnels that can be found 6.5 feet (2 m) below the surface of the earth and reach up to 2.5 miles (4 km) long.

What They Eat

Naked mole rats live their lives almost entirely underground and very rarely visit the surface. This means they eat food that's found under the earth, such as roots, stems, and plant bulbs (otherwise known as tubers). These treats are collected by the worker rats and brought back to the colony for the other rats and the queen to feast on.

Conservation Status

LEAST CONCERN

The naked mole rat lives across a relatively wide area, and their numbers seem to be growing. Their underground habitat is essentially untouched. But since they eat root vegetables, farmers will treat them as pests if there are too many of them around, taking off with all the beets and turnips!

FUN FACTS

✳ Naked mole rats can survive without air for up to 18 minutes.

✳ They can run backward just as fast as they can run forward!

✳ They've been documented to live to 30 years old in captivity. In fact, this species lives longer than any other rodent.

✳ They don't need to drink as their tuber-based diet keeps them well hydrated.

✳ To absorb as many nutrients as possible from a single meal, the rats will often eat each other's poo!

NORTH SULAWESI BABIRUSA

Babyrousa celebensis

(bab-uh-roo-sa sel-eb-en-sis)

Visible only on male babirusas, the long, curly tusks of this giant mammal are its most peculiar feature. Females have them, too—but theirs are a lot smaller and stay hidden in their mouths. The tusks are actually the male's upper canine teeth!

Males probably grow their tusks for display rather than combat. They're too thin and brittle to withstand much force. When male babirusas fight, they don't clash tusks—instead, they stand on their hind legs and box each other.

Their tusks grow throughout their lives and can reach 17 inches (43 cm) long. Sometimes the tusks will even grow through a babirusa's skull if they aren't worn down or broken off in a battle.

The babirusa has hairless, wrinkly skin. It's also exceptionally large, weighing around 130 to 220 pounds (60–100 kg) when fully grown.

Where They Live

Like their name suggests, these babirusas live primarily in Sulawesi, Indonesia. In the past, they enjoyed living in low-lying areas around riverbanks and rain forests, where they could find many different kinds of food. But thanks to heavy hunting and habitat destruction, they've moved to higher ground, which is safer because it's harder to get to.

What They Eat

Babirusas have such fierce-looking tusks, you'd expect them to hunt and eat large, intimidating beasts. But this isn't the case at all! They forage through sand and mud for leaves, fruits, roots, insects, fish, and small animals, and use their powerful jaws to crack nuts.

Conservation Status

VULNERABLE

Unfortunately, Sulawesi babirusas are among the first species to disappear from the ecosystem because of logging and deforestation. As their habitat is destroyed, their large size makes them easy to spot, and people love to hunt them for their meat and tusks. Their numbers have dropped by 30 percent in the past 20 years, and another 10 percent of them are expected to die out the near future.

FUN FACTS

❋ Babirusas are members of the swine family, which means they're related—though only distantly—to pigs, hogs, and boars.

❋ When they see familiar faces that they associate with food or fun, they'll wag their tails and jump around playfully, like a dog greeting its owner!

❋ They live to be around 24 years old.

❋ *Babirusa* is a Malay term meaning "pig deer."

❋ For centuries, Indonesian masks and folk art have been inspired by the babirusa. There's even a drawing of a female babirusa in the Maros Pangkep caves that's at least 36,000 years old!

NORTHERN BALD IBIS

Geronticus eremita

(jer-on-tik-us erem-ita)

One look at this ibis will tell you how it got its name: its featherless head, which makes the bird rather more ugly than lovely.

As with other bald birds, this lack of plumage is either an adaptation that helps them stay healthy and clean or a way to attract a mate. Northern bald ibis can be 28 to 30 inches (70–80 cm) tall and weigh around 2.5 pounds (1 kg). Their bodies are covered in iridescent feathers, which shift in hue from black to green to purple and are so alluring they almost make up for the bird's unsightly pink and grey noggin.

Where They Live

The northern bald ibis was originally native to the Middle East, central Europe, and North Africa, but now you'll only be able to spot them in Turkey, Syria, and Morocco. They live in a variety of habitats, ranging from natural areas, such as wetlands, fields, trees, and cliff edges, to man-made sites like rock walls and old castles.

What They Eat

This type of ibis sustains itself on many kinds of plants, berries and roots, as well as small animals such as worms, snakes, insects, fish, and amphibians. Occasionally they'll even feast on rodents and other birds.

Close Relations

The northern bald ibis is closely related to the much more common Australian white ibis, *Threskiornis moluccus* (page 22). It's easy to see the family resemblance in the shape of their body and beak.

Conservation Status

CRITICALLY ENDANGERED

The already small population of northern bald ibis has been drastically reduced by trophy hunting and the ever-increasing presence of humans. Massive numbers of these birds recently died in Turkey, where they were poisoned by pesticides meant to control mosquitoes and locusts.

FUN FACTS

❋ For birds, these ibis live for a relatively long time, sometimes reaching 25 years old.

❋ A group of ibis is called a congregation.

❋ Their nostrils are located at the base of their long beak, which allows them to keep breathing even while poking their beak into the mud to look for food.

❋ Other names for this bird include the waldrapp and the hermit ibis.

NORTHERN GROUND-HORNBILL

Bucorvus abyssinicus

(buk-or-vus ab-is-in-e-kus)

Hornbills are known for being large birds, but the ground-hornbill is much larger than the others, reaching around 4 feet (130 cm) long and weighing around 8 pounds (4 kg). They also have long, lanky legs to help them walk long distances. There are two species of ground-hornbill— the southern ground-hornbill and the northern ground-hornbill—each just as unusual as the other. Aside from their slightly different names, they also look a little different. For instance, the northern ground-hornbill's throat is blue and red, and it has blue patterning around its eyes.

Their large casques, or horns, aren't quite the same, either: The northern ground-hornbill's casque is curvier and features extra embellishments, like the bulky tube-shaped portion on top.

Where They Live

Their name gives it away—these hornbills spend most of their time on the ground. You'll track them down in dry, rocky parts of northeastern Africa, such as Kenya, Uganda, Ethiopia, and Somalia. At night, they roost in the holes of trees or stumps, or in rock crevices.

What They Eat

Unlike helmeted hornbills, ground-hornbills are carnivorous, which means they mainly eat animals. Their beaks didn't evolve to eat fruits or plants, so insects and spiders make up most of their meals—though sometimes they catch reptiles like lizards and snakes, or even small mammals.

Close Relations

They are related to the helmeted hornbill (page 62), which has a similar bony casque.

Conservation Status

LEAST CONCERN

Northern ground-hornbills have a wide range and large numbers, so they're not considered to be in danger of extinction. However, they still face threats, such as being eaten by large mammals or dying from disease. Occasionally humans will hunt them for food or kill them because they're seen as pests or symbols of bad luck.

FUN FACTS

✳ Northern ground-hornbills are monogamous, which means they mate for life. They like to sing duets with their partners, a touching display that's inspired their human neighbors to compose songs about them.

✳ Researchers have recorded them using their bills to wrestle with one another, but it seems to be a way for them to practice their hunting techniques rather than an act of aggression.

✳ In captivity, they can live as long as 40 years!

✳ They're also known as the Abyssinian ground-hornbill.

OCEAN SUNFISH

Mola mola

(mole-a mole-a)

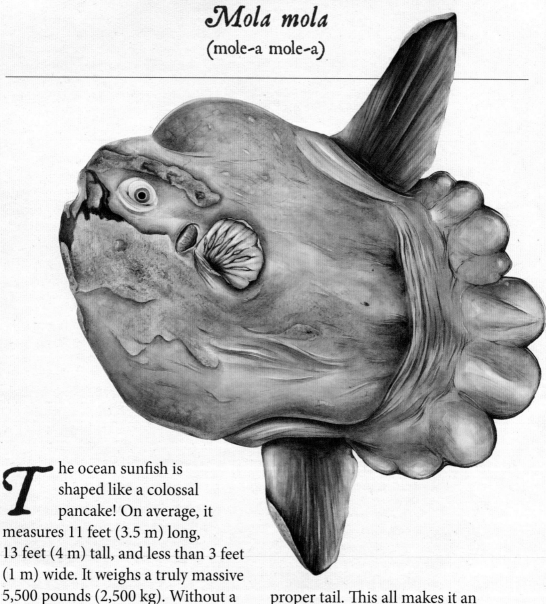

*T*he ocean sunfish is shaped like a colossal pancake! On average, it measures 11 feet (3.5 m) long, 13 feet (4 m) tall, and less than 3 feet (1 m) wide. It weighs a truly massive 5,500 pounds (2,500 kg). Without a swim bladder to help control its buoyancy, like other fish, it uses a layer of fat instead. It also lacks a proper tail. This all makes it an endearingly awkward, ungainly fish. The ocean sunfish is the heaviest bony fish in the world.

Where They Live

Ocean sunfish live in a wide range of waters, from the central coast of New South Wales in Australia all the way up to the Mediterranean Sea. They spend most of their time at great depths, but sometimes they'll swim to the surface to regulate their body temperature or let other fish and birds pluck parasites off their skin while they float on one side, soaking up some sunshine.

What They Eat

Ocean sunfish are omnivorous, which means they'll eat both plants and animals. They're especially fond of jellyfish and plankton, though on occasion they'll sample other fish and crustaceans. They tend to eat small animals because their mouths are tiny compared to their large body, and they're not able to close them completely.

Close Relations

This enormous fish is closely related to the tiny pufferfish in the family Tetraodontidae.

Conservation Status

VULNERABLE

Lots of creatures hunt the ocean sunfish, including orcas, sea lions, and great white sharks. After all, they're big enough to make an epic feast for anything that catches them! But humans are the biggest threat to this fish. Many sunfish die after being struck by boats or caught in fishing nets. Many more die from eating plastic waste, which they mistake for jellyfish. In one year alone, people caught around 340,000 sunfish, either by accident or on purpose.

FUN FACTS

✳ They can live for up to 10 years.

✳ They have many nicknames, including "swimming head" and "moon fish."

✳ Their scientific name, *Mola mola*, comes from the Latin word for "millstone"—a grey, circular disc used to grind wheat and other grains. Apparently, they look a little like a millstone (a swimming millstone, that is).

✳ These fish take it slow: Their fastest recorded speed is only around 2 miles (3 km) per hour!

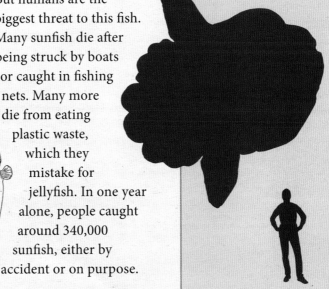

PROBOSCIS MONKEY

Nasalis larvatus

(nay-sa-lis lar-vat-us)

The proboscis monkey has a nose like no other monkey, but nobody knows why it has such a nose! Scientists believe it may have something to do with finding mates. The larger a male's nose, the more attractive he is to females. Males also use their nose to make loud noises that entice females while warning other males to stay away.

Male proboscis monkeys weigh around 45 pounds (20 kg) and can grow to 30 inches (80 cm) tall. The females are smaller, weighing about 22 pounds (10 kg) and growing to 24 inches (60 cm) tall. Females also have a much shorter snout that turns up at the end.

Where They Live

Found only on the island of Borneo, these mammals live in groups of around 20 individuals, with one male and many females. They are arboreal, which means they spend most of their days and nights high in the trees of forests, swamps, and mangroves, only coming down to cross rivers or feed on fallen food.

Conservation Status

ENDANGERED

Sadly, these peculiar monkeys have lost more than 50 percent of their population in the past 40 years. Palm oil plantations are the leading cause of this tremendous loss. Over 27,000 square miles (70,000 sq km) of their habitat has been cleared for palm plantations.

What They Eat

These monkeys love to eat the leaves and sour, star-shaped fruit of a tree called the crabapple mangrove. They'll also feast on seeds, roots, shoots, and, on occasion, insects.

FUN FACTS

❋ Proboscis monkeys are excellent swimmers! They have webbed hands and feet that help them paddle through the water from mangrove to mangrove.

❋ A group of proboscis monkeys is called a harem.

❋ They are an easygoing species and rarely fight each other for dominance.

❋ You can help save the proboscis monkey from extinction by doing two things: limiting your consumption of palm oil, which is used in food, cosmetics, and gasoline; and raising awareness about the impact of deforestation.

❋ Proboscis monkeys have chambered stomachs for digesting leaves, which is why they have such amazingly round bellies!

❋ The Malay nickname for these monkeys is *orang belanda*, or "Dutchman."

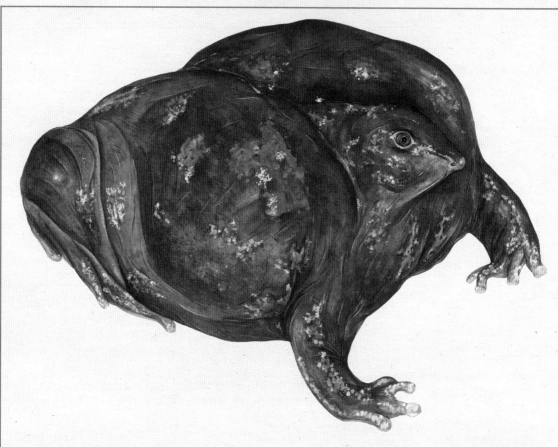

PURPLE PIG-NOSED FROG

Nasikabatrachus sahyadrensis

(nay-sik-a-bat-rak-us sah-hya-dren-sis)

Purple pig-nosed frogs are petite amphibians: only 2 to 3.5 inches (6–9 cm) long. They weigh a mere 6 ounces (165 g) and have bulbous bodies and strange pointy snouts. Their heads appear to be too small for the rest of them!

These frogs live underground, and their long noses are perfect for digging, while their short limbs, with hard knobs on the back feet, are ideal for pushing dirt aside. When they eat, their tongues poke out of their flexible, flap-like lower jaw.

Where They Live

The purple pig-nosed frog can be found in the Western Ghats, a mountain range in India, in the damp, loose soil of forests and other areas with dense plant life. They spend most of their lives as deep as 3 feet (1 m) underground. If you're lucky enough to visit their territory during monsoon season, you can spot them in pond-like environments where they breed for a few weeks of the year.

What They Eat

Since these frogs spend most of their time underground, they've developed some specific traits to help them find food there. They have a sensitive nose and mouth that allow them to catch and eat small invertebrates and termites, and their tongues are specially designed to stick to and suck up these insects, making the purple frog a very quick eater.

Conservation Status

ENDANGERED

This bizarre species of frog is extremely rare—only 135 of them have been found in the wild, and only 3 of those were female! In fact, scientists didn't even recognize this species until 2003, although local people knew about the frogs and had even named them. They may have remained so obscure because they're burrowing frogs, rarely seen aboveground. This also makes it difficult to know exactly where they live, how many of them there are, and what threats they face. However, deforestation probably presents the biggest threat to the purple pig-nosed frog. Ninety percent of their forest home has been logged, mostly to make way for farm crops like ginger, coffee, and cardamom.

FUN FACTS

* Female purple pig-nosed frogs are much larger than males, which is an unusual form of sexual dimorphism for most kinds of animals, but not for frogs.

* Researchers monitored a purple frog closely for five months—it didn't emerge from its burrow once in that entire time!

* While still a tadpole, the pig-nosed frog will sometimes crawl out of the water to feed at night, even though it doesn't have any limbs. They use their strong abdominal muscles to move from one tiny pocket of water to another.

RED-LIPPED BATFISH

Ogcocephalus darwini

(og-ko-sef-a-lus dar-win-e)

*T*he vibrant red lips of this unusual batfish look like they're covered in freshly applied lipstick. Why these fish have evolved to have such dramatic lips is a mystery, but it might help males attract females during mating season, or it may help them recognize other batfish.

Still, the red-lipped batfish probably won't be winning any beauty contests—or any swim meets, either! They're not especially strong swimmers and often rely on their leg-shaped fins to walk across the seabed.

Since they don't swim well enough to catch their dinner, they beckon their meals to come to them with their illicium, a retractable lure under their elongated snout that wiggles about like a small fish and releases chemicals to entice nearby prey to swim closer.

These batfish grow to around 10 inches (25 cm) long.

Where They Live

They live almost exclusively around the Galápagos Islands, in the Pacific Ocean off the coast of South America, but sometimes they turn up in waters closer to Ecuador and Peru. They like to dwell on sandy floors between 10 and 250 feet (3–75 m) below sea level, but have been found as far as 395 feet (120 m) deep.

What They Eat

Their lure helps them catch plenty of small fish and such tasty invertebrates as crabs, mollusks, and shrimp.

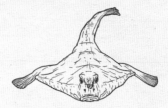

Close Relations

This species is a kind of anglerfish, like the humpback anglerfish (page 64). Both fish have an illicium that they can use to attract prey. But the red-lipped batfish's lure doesn't light up like the humpback anglerfish's does.

Conservation Status

LEAST CONCERN

The batfish lives in such a unique habitat that environmental changes don't affect it in the same way as many other ocean-dwelling species. Deep-sea trawlers may occasionally drag these fish up to the surface or destroy their homes on the seabed, but since they live mostly within the protected waters of the Galápagos Marine Reserve, their population numbers are stable.

RETICULATE STARGAZER

Dactyloscopus foraminosus
(dak-til-o-sco-pus for-a-mi-no-sus)

*W*hat would it be like to have eyes on the top of your head? Just ask the reticulate stargazer. This flattened, zombie-faced fish can lie on the marine floor without moving and keep an eye on its surroundings.

These fish are easy to miss, but that's how they like it! Reaching 3 inches (8 cm) long at most, they have speckled skin that helps them blend in with their surroundings, and their large side fins do a great job of digging up the sand around them so they can bury themselves in seconds.

Where They Live

They like to hide in the sand and gravel of marine waters, so reticulate stargazers aren't easy to spot. If you'd like to try your luck finding one, though, you'd best start your search in certain parts of the western Atlantic—such as the waters off the coast of Brazil—at depths of around 36 to 260 feet (11–80 m).

What They Eat

This unusual fish has some very interesting traits that have evolved to help it hunt and feed on crabs, small fish, and squid. They attract prey with a worm-like lure above their mouth, dangling it around and then lurching forward to swallow their victims. They use fringe-like appendages on the outside of their mouth to stop any unwanted sand and debris from getting in.

Conservation Status

LEAST CONCERN

Reticulate stargazers face very little danger during their lives, as they spend most of their time beneath the marine floor, hidden from any potential threats. Some fishermen consider the fish to be a delicacy, but most keep their distance because, when threatened, this fish is likely to sting or even electrocute you.

FUN FACTS

✳ Don't mess with a stargazer! They have two venomous spines on their back and an organ behind their eyes that can send out an electrical shock of up to 50 volts.

✳ They're called stargazers because their eyes face straight up, so they're always looking toward the sky.

✳ Often they'll burp up the scales of the fish they've just snacked on.

✳ There are nearly 50 different species of stargazer!

SAIGA ANTELOPE

Saiga tatarica

(sigh-ga tat-a-reek-a)

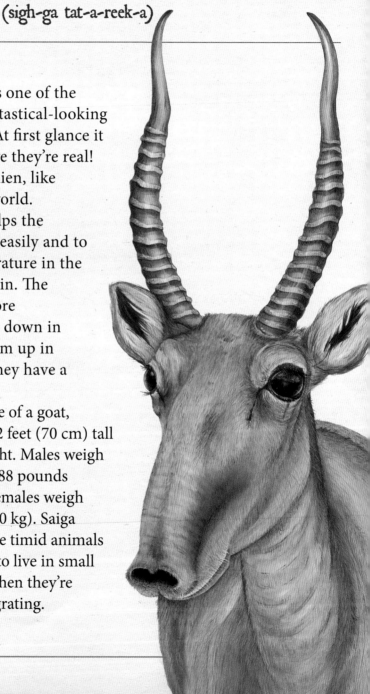

This little antelope is one of the strangest, most fantastical-looking animals on earth. At first glance it may even be hard to believe they're real! Their noses seem almost alien, like something from another world.

The saiga's long snout helps the antelopes to breathe more easily and to regulate their body temperature in the extreme climates they live in. The larger their nose is, the more efficiently it can cool them down in the summer and warm them up in the winter. It also means they have a superb sense of smell!

They're only about the size of a goat, standing around 2 feet (70 cm) tall at shoulder height. Males weigh approximately 88 pounds (40 kg) and females weigh 66 pounds (30 kg). Saiga antelope are timid animals that like to live in small herds when they're not migrating.

Where They Live

Saiga are very rare these days, but if you want to find one, you'll have to travel to Mongolia, Russia, or Kazakhstan. Their population is dwindling fast, and in some places they haven't been seen in 40 years. Every year in November, they migrate long distances in search of areas with enough low-lying trees and plants to eat all winter. More than 10,000 saiga will travel together on these taxing journeys. They prefer wide open spaces to dense, overgrown habitat, where it would be harder for them to escape from predators.

What They Eat

Saiga antelope usually eat grass, shrubs, lichen, and herbs. They can also eat some plants that are poisonous to other animals without getting sick.

Conservation Status

CRITICALLY ENDANGERED

In the past 40 years, more than a million saiga have died, leaving only around 50,000 left in the wild—a catastrophic loss. They once lived throughout China and Ukraine, but no longer. Humans hunt male saiga in large numbers for their highly prized meat and horns. This means there are fewer males for the females to breed with, which means fewer babies are born each year. The World Wildlife Fund has listed these critically endangered animals as a priority species to try to prevent them from becoming entirely extinct.

FUN FACTS

✳ During mating season, the heated fights the saiga antelope get into can be deadly. The antelopes can seriously harm one another with their horns.

✳ A saiga can live for up to 10 years.

✳ These speedy animals frighten easily and can run up to 50 miles (80 km) per hour to escape predators.

✳ Do you notice the saiga's very large eyes? These antelopes rely on their keen eyesight to look out for danger. Many other kinds of antelope rely on their hearing.

✳ Saiga have been around since the last Ice Age, about 18,000 years ago, when they roamed in large numbers across almost all of what is now Asia and Europe, alongside woolly mammoths and saber-toothed cats.

SANTIAGO GIANT TORTOISE

Chelonoidis darwini
(kel-o-noy-dis dar-win-e)

Compared to the small, cute turtles that most people are familiar with, giant tortoises may seem ugly and intimidating. Their skin and carapace, or shell, are a dull grey color, and they have deep wrinkles on their neck, head, and feet.

These tortoises have very long necks, so they can munch on tall plants. They're also useful during confrontations with other tortoises, when the animals will face one another with their necks fully extended and their mouths open wide.

Because of the hot climates they live in and their minimal need for food, Santiago giant tortoises spend the majority of their time sleeping and resting, sometimes for weeks at a time!

Where They Live

These tortoises are native to Ecuador, and you can find them on the Galápagos Island of Santiago, previously known as James Island.

What They Eat

Because they're able to store water in their bladders, these incredible animals can survive a whole year without food and water! When they do eat, they'll munch on grass, fruit, and sometimes cactus pads.

Conservation Status

CRITICALLY ENDANGERED

The Santiago giant tortoise once lived comfortably on the Galápagos Islands but is now on the brink of extinction. When humans introduced non-native animals like goats, pigs, and donkeys to the Galápagos in the seventeenth century, the tortoises' home came under threat because of overgrazing. Plus, both humans and animals would steal and eat the tortoises' eggs. More recently, the goats were removed from the islands, but then invasive plants, like blackberry bushes, grew out of control, further endangering the tortoises' habitat.

FUN FACTS

* The Santiago giant tortoise can live to be more than 150 years old!

* Tortoises may have first arrived on the Galápagos Islands around 2 to 3 million years ago from the coast of South America, via rafts made from vegetation.

* Female tortoises lay their eggs in nests of sand or soil. The temperature of the nest determines whether the baby tortoises will be female or male.

* Around 165 years ago, Charles Darwin brought a young Santiago giant tortoise named Harriet from the Galápagos to Australia. Harriet spent part of her life at Australia Zoo. She died there in 2006, at the grand old age of 175 years old (give or take)!

SARCASTIC FRINGEHEAD

Neoclinus blanchardi

(ne-o-kline-us blan-char-dee)

You don't want to come across a sarcastic fringehead while taking a swim. Not only do they have a terrifying mouth filled with needle-sharp teeth, they're also not the friendliest fish in the sea.

When they feel threatened, they'll flash their large mouth and teeth as a warning, but then they'll go on the attack if they think there's still a threat. They'll even attack humans! Because they're so fierce, they have very few predators, despite being relatively small—only around 10 inches (25 cm) long.

Male fringeheads use a similar approach when they compete with other males for a mate—they'll open their mouth wide to try and dominate each other. Sometimes they'll lunge at each other, bumping heads to intimidate their opponent, with the loser retreating.

What They Eat

These omnivorous fish live so deep in the sea that we don't know much about what they eat, but their diets probably consist of small plankton, fish, crustaceans, and squid and their eggs.

Conservation Status

LEAST CONCERN

Like the red-lipped batfish (page 96), this fish spends its days deep in the ocean where fishermen or trawlers rarely catch it and where water pollution has less impact. Since the fringehead also happens to live in protected areas, its population is not considered to be at risk.

Where They Live

Sarcastic fringeheads enjoy the subtropical climate of the eastern Pacific Ocean and live off the coast of California and Mexico. They spend their time on sandy or muddy seafloors as deep as 195 feet (60 m) below the surface, and they like to rest in burrows or in large shells left behind by other creatures.

FUN FACTS

* Sarcastic fringeheads sometimes make their homes in plastic bottles or other garbage that's made its way into the ocean.

* Their unusual name comes from the original Greek meaning of the word *sarcastic*: "to tear flesh."

* Fishermen don't usually try to catch fringeheads because they're such aggressive fish.

* They consume nearly 14 times their body weight in food every year!

* Female fringeheads lay their eggs in abandoned burrows dug out by other animals, and males stand guard to protect the eggs from any hungry visitors.

SEA LAMPREY

Petromyzon marinus

(Pet-ro-my-zon ma-reen-us)

These snake-like creatures are often mistaken for eels when they're seen swimming through the water. The major difference between the two species is that lampreys have circular mouths filled with multiple rows of large teeth. Rather than biting and swallowing their prey, sea lampreys are parasitic feeders: They attach themselves to other fish with their teeth and suck their host's blood and nutrients—like an underwater vampire! They're usually around 3 feet long (1 m) and can weigh up to 5.5 pounds (2.5 kg).

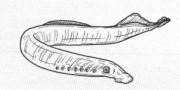

Where They Live

Sea lampreys can be found in the Atlantic Ocean, in the waters surrounding Iceland, and in the western Mediterranean Sea. They've also been introduced to many other areas, often causing harm to local marine life in the process. The sea lamprey can travel between bodies of water that have different salinities, or levels of salt. This makes them quite unusual—very few species of fish are able to survive in both saltwater and freshwater environments. In adulthood, they migrate from the ocean into rivers so they can reproduce.

What They Eat

Catfish, salmon, and rainbow trout are some of the fish the sea lamprey likes to feed on. A single lamprey can kill up to 40 pounds (18 kg) of these fish in its lifetime! Lampreys spend most of their days in groups, attaching to different hosts, but once they reach sexual maturity, they stop feeding altogether.

Conservation Status

LEAST CONCERN

Sea lampreys are seen as invasive pests by many people because of their negative impact on other fish, particularly those that are bought and sold for food around the globe. In fact, there's an official program in place to decrease their numbers, with traps set up in the Great Lakes region of North America to keep the lamprey from causing further damage to other fish. It's the only animal in this book that conservationists are actively trying to get rid of.

FUN FACTS

* They're also known as spotted lamprey and green lamprey.

* Sea lampreys can live to be five years old.

* Their skeletons are made entirely of cartilage rather than bone.

* A female lamprey can lay between 30,000 and 100,000 eggs when spawning.

* Young lampreys are blind and don't have any teeth!

SOUTHERN CASSOWARY

Casuarius casuarius

(cas-oo-ar-ee-us cas-oo-ar-ee-us)

T he southern cassowary's large, horn-like helmet, also known as a casque, is surprisingly soft inside. This impressive headpiece begins to grow when the bird is one or two years old. It evolved over thousands of years to help them push through the dense foliage of the rain forest as they walk around—like their ostrich and emu relatives, southern cassowaries can't fly!

They have not one but two dangling red wattles on their necks, which can intensify in color when the bird is enraged or excited. Weighing in at roughly 165 pounds (75 kg), females are heavier than males and can grow to 6.5 feet (2 m) tall. The males get to around 120 pounds (55 kg).

Where They Live

The southern cassowary is native to Australia, eastern Indonesia, and Papua New Guinea, but you'll have the best chance of seeing them in the wild in the rain forests of northern Queensland. Now and then they'll hang out on beaches and in mangrove stands, woodlands, and swamps.

What They Eat

These large birds feed mainly on fallen fruit and fungi, and they poo out the seeds from the fruits they eat, helping new trees and bushes grow. That's why they're known as the best seed distributors in the rain forest! They also dine on small animals like snails and fish from time to time.

Conservation Status

LEAST CONCERN

The southern cassowary doesn't have many predators, except for dogs and feral pigs. However, their numbers are threatened by car collisions, hunting, and land clearing for logging and palm oil plantations.

FUN FACTS

* The southern cassowary is the heaviest non-flying bird in Australia.

* Because of their powerful legs, they can run at speeds of 31 miles (50 km) per hour and jump 5 feet (1.5 m) high!

* The male cassowary sits on the eggs—which are green!—to warm and protect them.

* One of the easiest ways to tell whether a cassowary is male or female is to measure the size of its three-toed feet. A female's feet are over 8 inches (20 cm) long, while a male's are shorter.

* Do you know why the cassowary plum, *Cerbera floribunda*, is named after this bird? Well, it's one of the cassowary's favorite foods. And it has the same vibrant blue color that makes the bird so stunning.

SOUTHERN ELEPHANT SEAL

Mirounga leonina

(mi-rung-ga lee-oh-ni-na)

Southern elephant seals are the largest carnivores living today! Females can grow to 1,765 pounds (800 kg) and 13 feet (4 m) long, while males can reach an even more massive 8,820 pounds (4,000 kg) and 20 feet (6 m) long.

The males have a funny, trunk-like nose, which overhangs their face by about 4 inches (10 cm). This trunk doubles as an amplifier when it's inflated, allowing the seals' calls to be heard far and wide. To help show who's boss, males will also make loud bellowing sounds during fights.

Males need to defend their harems—the females they've mated with—so they'll stay put in their territory for months on end. This means they're not able to go hunt for food, which wears them out over time. Only the strongest males can make it, so they're the ones that are able to breed and pass on their genes.

Where They Live

These humongous mammals make their homes in the cold waters around Antarctica and near subantarctic islands, but they've also been spotted a handful of times in Australia, New Zealand, and South Africa. It's hard to know exactly where they go and how far they travel—when it's not mating season, these seals spend most of their time at sea rather than on land.

What They Eat

Because of how big they are, southern elephant seals can hunt and eat large animals like sharks, large fish, and squid. They can dive so deep—over 4,920 feet (1,500 m)—that they may even dine on elusive, mysterious deep-sea creatures. But since they catch their prey while swimming far out at sea, no one knows for sure.

Conservation Status

LEAST CONCERN

Around 30 years ago, there were about 650,000 southern elephant seals in the world. Since then, their numbers have dropped, probably because of climate change and overfishing. Other threats to these enormous seals are few and far between. Sometimes they're hunted by killer whales, great white sharks, and leopard seals, which prey mainly on the smaller pups.

FUN FACTS

* Southern elephant seals can live as many as 23 years in the wild.

* They're able to hold their breath underwater for up to two hours!

* This species of seal has lived on the earth for around a million years.

* Even though they can travel up to 3,100 miles (5,000 km) to find good feeding waters, elephant seals will return to the place they were born in order to breed.

* Before 1964, elephant seals were hunted for their blubber, which was used for oil.

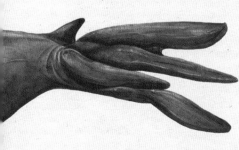

STAR-NOSED MOLE

Condylura cristata

(con-de-lure-a cris-ta-ta)

*D*oes this mole have a rosy red flower stuck to its face? Or a pink, rubbery sea anemone? No—that's its nose! Shaped like a star with 22 points, or rays, the nose of the star-nosed mole is utterly unique. Most noses are good at picking up smells, but this one helps the mole feel things as it searches for prey and digs underground tunnels.

How does it do this? The mole's nose is packed with over 25,000 sensory receptors known as Eimer's organs. Using these organs, they can feel different objects in tremendous detail, sensing the microscopic texture of everything they touch. Since the star-nosed mole is basically blind, this is a huge help to them. And it all happens very fast: Their

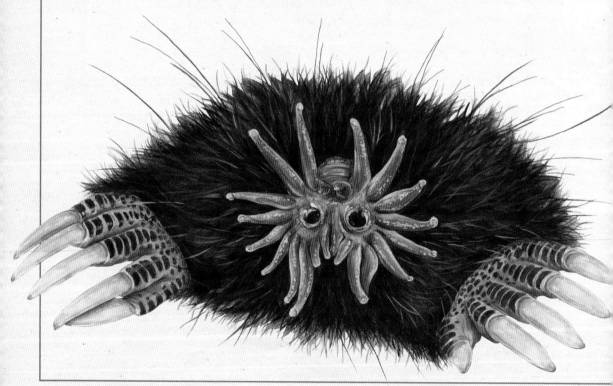

nose moves around so quickly that it can touch up to 12 objects every second!

The star-nosed mole grows to between 7 and 8 inches (17.5–20 cm) long, with a 0.25-inch-long (7 mm) tail that's covered in scales and coarse hair.

Where They Live

These critters are native to the northeastern United States, but can also be found in parts of Canada, living farther north than any other kind of mole. They like to inhabit wetlands, like the clearings and meadows near riverbanks, lakes, and ponds.

To find them, you'll need to look for mole hills, the mounds of dirt piled outside their tunnels. Their intricate tunnel networks can reach 885 feet (270 m) long.

What They Eat

These moles are the world's fastest eaters. Once they've located their prey with their incredible noses, they can devour foods like worms, insects, fish, and crustaceans in just a quarter of a second!

Close Relations

This species is related to the naked mole rat (page 82), which also lives in long, sophisticated tunnel networks.

Conservation Status

LEAST CONCERN

Star-nosed moles have a few natural predators: fish, bullfrogs, and large birds, like owls. They're also hunted by more invasive species, like domesticated cats and dogs, and, like almost all animals, they suffer from the effects of human expansion into their environment. However, these threats don't impact them enough to put them at risk of extinction.

FUN FACTS

✱ Star-nosed moles can smell underwater! When they wade or swim, they blow air bubbles out of their nose, then inhale them again. This lets them sniff out prey in the surrounding water. We know of only one other mammal that's able to do this—the water shrew.

✱ A group of moles is called a labor.

✱ Eimer's organs are filled with so many sensory nerves that the star-nosed mole's nose is five times more sensitive than the human hand!

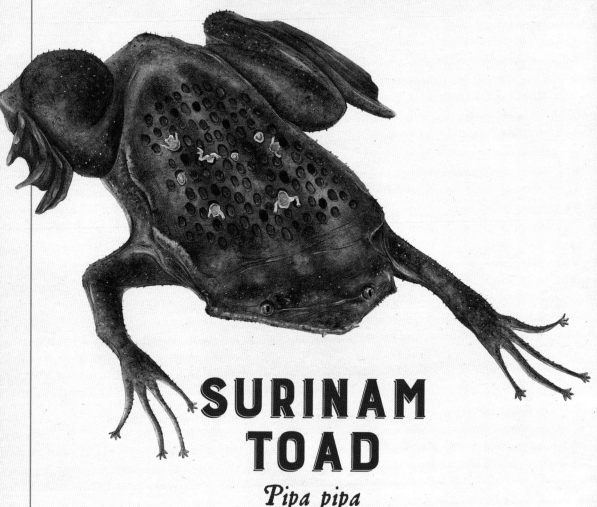

SURINAM TOAD

Pipa pipa
(pip-a pip-a)

What are those spots on the back of the Surinam toad? Believe it or not, they're small holes, and each one contains a baby toad! These bizarre amphibians have a remarkable ability: They incubate and hatch their babies in their backs. This way, they can protect their eggs from predators, which they wouldn't be able to do as well if they laid the eggs on a rock or in the water. When they mate, the eggs are implanted in the female's back, and afterward she grows a layer of skin over them. After 12 to 20 weeks, tiny toads emerge!

Surinam toads are so flat, they look like they've been stepped on or run over. Males average around 4 to 6 inches (10–15 cm) long and females are a little bigger.

Where They Live

This toad gets its name from one of the places it calls home: Suriname. You'll also find them in the Amazon basin of South America, in such countries as Bolivia, Ecuador, Colombia, Brazil, and Trinidad and Tobago. They can be difficult to spot as they're extremely flat and conceal themselves well in their rain-forest habitat. Tucked under debris or dirt in ponds, rivers, and pools of water, they look just like fallen leaves or flat rocks.

What They Eat

Unlike most frogs and toads, the Surinam toad doesn't have a tongue! Instead it relies on its star-like fingers to sense food nearby and shove it into its mouth. It also uses suction to swallow passing snacks in one gulp.

Surinam toads usually find worms, small fish, invertebrates, and crustaceans this way, but they're not fussy eaters and will gobble up almost anything they come across—even other Surinam toads!

Conservation Status

LEAST CONCERN

Surinam toads are occasionally collected and sold as pets, but habitat loss is their main threat. Although many of the places they live are protected, they still fall victim to logging, land-clearing for plantations, and the intrusion of humans. Fortunately, there are lots of them around right now, and they're not at risk of extinction in the near future.

TARDIGRADE

Tardigrada

(tar-di-grad-a)

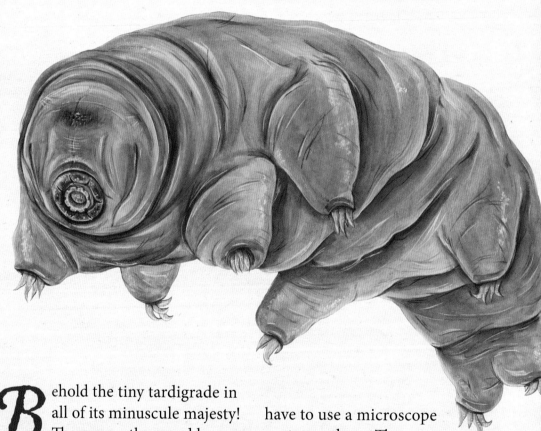

Behold the tiny tardigrade in all of its minuscule majesty! There are a thousand known species of tardigrade in the world, and all of them are so small—measuring only 0.005 to 0.12 centimeters (0.05–1.2 mm)—that you have to use a microscope to see them. They have a barrel-shaped body, a tube-like mouthpart, and four pairs of stubby legs with claws on the ends.

These weird-looking invertebrates don't need a mate to reproduce, so if they can't find one, they can still have baby tardigrades. Some females can basically clone themselves, while others are actually hermaphroditic—possessing both sexes—and can fertilize their own eggs.

Where They Live

These astonishing creatures are able to survive in conditions that many of us could never dream of. For example, they can handle truly extreme temperatures, from around −455°F (−270°C), far below freezing, up to the scorching heat of 300°F (150°C). They've even survived in outer space by placing their bodies into a dormant state known as cryptobiosis.

Found all around the world, from the Arctic to the Antarctic, tardigrades live in all kinds of environments—oceans, sand, rivers, rain forests, mossy tree trunks. In fact, there may very well be some in your backyard right now!

What They Eat

Their tube-like mouths are filled with sharp teeth that they use to suck the juices from the cells of moss, algae, and bacteria. Sometimes they'll even feast on fellow tardigrades.

Conservation Status

NOT EVALUATED

These creatures are so small that it's impossible to count them or figure out exactly where they live, so people haven't been able to determine whether they're threatened or not. Because they're so tiny and also so tough, they probably don't have many predators—just spiders, crustaceans, mites, snails, and other tardigrades. Of course, climate change may endanger the tardigrade.

FUN FACTS

✳ Depending on their diet, their colors can range from brown to orange to pink to yellow to green. They can even be transparent!

✳ They're also known as moss piglets and water bears.

✳ One specimen survived over 30 years in its dormant state.

✳ A tardigrade can usually live between three months and two and a half years.

✳ These animals are so resilient, they've survived five mass extinctions over the past 500 million years.

.005–0.12 cm

TURKEY VULTURE

Cathartes aura
(kath-ar-teez or-a)

Like most vultures, this enormous bird is bald. While this means they may never be as cute as a cockatoo, it does mean they can feast on their favorite food—carrion—without the risk of getting bits of dead animals stuck to their head. Plus, it would be a waste of time and effort to have to clean their feathers after every meal—they'll only get dirty again at dinner!

Turkey vultures have a massive wingspan of nearly 6.5 feet (2 m), yet they're incredibly light, weighing only around 3 to 4 pounds (1.5–2 kg). They are larger than hawks, but smaller than eagles and condors. Most of their feathers are a glossy brownish-black color. Their hooked ivory beaks help them tear meat off carcasses.

Where They Live

Turkey vultures live throughout much of North and South America, including Canada, Chile, and parts of the United States, like Texas and Minnesota. In the winter, they migrate to warmer climates. Where they roost depends on where they're feeding at the time, which can vary from forests to fields to deserts to coasts, in trees, cliffs, or man-made structures.

What They Eat

What might taste revolting to us is what's tastiest to a turkey vulture! Like marabou storks (page 76), these raptors eat mostly carrion. This means they feed on animals that are already dead and have often started to decay, including roadkill, cattle, and smaller birds. Sometimes they'll eat insects or fruit.

Scavenger birds like these are critically important to the earth's ecosystem because they clean up germ-ridden animal carcasses that might otherwise contaminate the water or soil.

Conservation Status

LEAST CONCERN

Turkey vultures have a creative way of deterring predators. If threatened, they'll throw up their last meal (which was almost always old, rotting meat). This gives off such a strong, foul odor that other animals won't stick around for long. Thanks to this stinky trick, they face few natural predators. Humans cause the most harm to this species, through trapping, shooting, and car accidents.

FUN FACTS

✳ To frighten off potential predators, turkey vultures will not only vomit, but also play dead—though this only works if the other animal isn't also a scavenger!

✳ If a turkey vulture is feeling threatened, it will make a hissing sound.

✳ Most birds can't smell very well, but the turkey vulture has an excellent sense of smell, which it uses to locate dead animals rather than relying purely on sight.

✳ Turkey vultures form strong bonds with their mates, and partnered birds will remain together for life.

✳ People have seen them sleeping in flocks as large as a few hundred birds, probably because there's safety in numbers.

VULTURINE GUINEAFOWL

Acryllium vulturinum

(a-krill-e-um vul-chur-e-num)

These guineafowl have featherless heads and necks, like vultures. But vultures are bald so they can feed on carcasses without their head feathers becoming filthy, while vulturine guineafowls mostly eat plants. They also sport a band of brown feathers on the back of their blue-grey heads.

Both sexes stand between 23 and 28 inches tall (60–72 cm) and weigh between 22 and 35 pounds (10–16 kg). They also have the same coloring, so it can be difficult to tell them apart by sight alone. They do behave differently, though—males fight one another over food, mates, and territory.

Males also carry themselves differently, trying to look as large and intimidating as possible to frighten off any competition for a female guineafowl's attention.

Where They Live

To see these birds in their natural habitat, you'll have to go to East Africa, where you'll find them in the tropical regions of Kenya, Ethiopia, Somalia, Uganda, and Tanzania.

They enjoy humid lowland forests and dry grasslands and live in large groups of around 25 individuals—safety in numbers!

What They Eat

These guineafowl usually dine on grass, leaves, roots, fruit, and seeds. Sometimes they'll eat insects, small reptiles, and scorpions, which they dig up from the ground with their sharp claws.

Conservation Status

LEAST CONCERN

These guineafowl are relatively plentiful, in part because they don't have many predators. However, they do have a few—for example, larger birds, monkeys, and pigs, which like to eat their eggs. And humans enjoy hunting them for their vibrant blue feathers, which are highly sought after.

FUN FACTS

* Although they have wings, vulturine guineafowl prefer to walk or run on the ground, even if they're frightened.

* They live to be around 15 years old.

* Usually females will share nests, lay their eggs together, and help each other look after the eggs.

* Of the six species of guineafowl, these are the tallest.

* Because they eat so many plants, they usually don't need to drink water—they get all the water they need from the plants!

WHITEMARGIN UNICORNFISH

Naso annulatus

(nay-so an-you-la-tus)

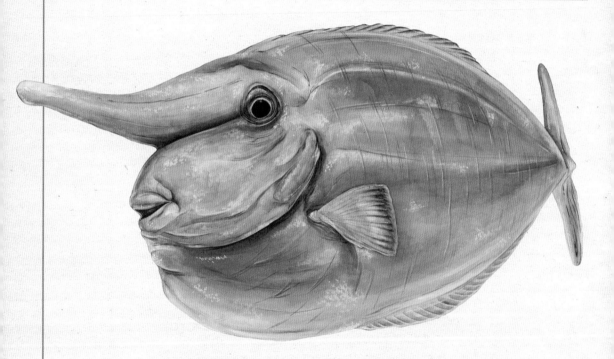

As you may have guessed, the unicornfish gets its name from the long proboscis, or snout, protruding from its forehead. These fish aren't born with these "horns"; instead, they start growing once the fish have reached around 8 inches (20 cm) long. The horn can grow as long as 5 inches (13 cm), and the fish itself will reach a maximum length of 3 feet (1 m).

This species is sexually dimorphic, and the males have much longer horns than the females. No one knows why they have them, but it does make them stand out in a crowd!

Where They Live

Happiest at depths of 65 to 195 feet (20–60 m), the whitemargin unicornfish lives in tropical waters throughout the Indo-Pacific region and often swims in schools around coral reefs. You'll also find them all along the Great Barrier Reef, Lord Howe Island, and other areas off the coast of Australia.

What They Eat

These fish are herbivores, or plant eaters. They use their small, sharp teeth to nibble algae off coral and rocks in the ocean, which is incredibly helpful because this algae may otherwise overgrow and kill the coral. Unicornfish also eat tiny plankton scattered throughout the ocean.

Close Relations

They are part of the surgeonfish family, like Dory from *Finding Nemo*! (Dory is a regal blue tang fish.)

Conservation Status

LEAST CONCERN

In the Philippines, whitemargin unicornfish are caught for food. Sometimes they're also taken to be sold as aquarium pets. As a result, their numbers have fallen over the years. However, these practices haven't had a huge impact on the fish, so they're not currently endangered.

FUN FACTS

✳ Whitemargin unicornfish have been recorded to reach the ripe old age of 23!

✳ As if having a unicorn horn wasn't special enough, they can also quickly change their color depending on their surroundings, or even their mood.

✳ They also go by the names ringtail unicornfish and short-horned unicornfish.

✳ At the base of their tail they have spines that are as sharp as daggers! They use these to defend themselves and to display dominance over other unicornfish.

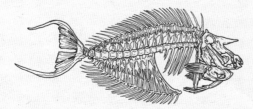

WILD TURKEY

Meleagris gallopavo
(mel-e-a-gris gal-o-pav-o)

Male and female wild turkeys are easy to tell apart. Males have a marvelous fan-shaped tail of coppery, iridescent feathers, a wrinkled red wattle at their throats, spurs on their legs that they use in combat, and a curious fleshy growth that drapes over their beak and head and is known as a snood or caruncle. This ugly facial feature has a very specific purpose—it changes in size and color based on how the bird is feeling. For instance, if a bird is feeling threatened or angry, or if it's ready to mate, the snood will become larger and darker in color. Males can reach weights of 15 to 24 pounds (7–11 kg), while female turkeys—called hens—usually weigh only 8 to 12 pounds (3.5–5.5 kg) and are much plainer than the males. Only male turkeys gobble. The sound attracts potential mates and warns any competing males to stay away.

Where They Live

Wild turkeys reside in forests, woodlands, pastures, and fields, where they spend most of their day grazing before roosting together in trees at night. You can find these turkeys throughout parts of the United States, Canada, and Mexico, but people have brought them to New Zealand, Australia, and Germany as well.

What They Eat

Like other turkeys, the wild turkey is an omnivore. They'll use their feet to scratch at vegetation on the ground, searching for insects, nuts, seeds, and leaves. Sometimes they'll even reach their beaks up to short trees and shrubs to peck off buds and fruit.

Conservation Status

LEAST CONCERN

The wild turkey is the most popular game bird in the United States and is the central ingredient in Thanksgiving dinner. So it's not surprising that each year, over 45 million turkeys are killed in the United States alone. But they're not at any risk of dying out—in fact, the number of wild turkeys in the world has increased by 18,700 percent in the past 40 years! After disappearing in many areas because of overhunting, they were reintroduced and have made a strong comeback. Humans aren't their only predator—wild turkeys are also hunted by foxes, raccoons, snakes, and rodents, who will all gladly make a meal of them or their eggs.

FUN FACTS

* Wild turkeys can live for 10 years, but since humans love to hunt them for food, most live to be just five or six months old.

* Their gobbles can be heard as far as a mile (1.5 km) away.

* Although these turkeys often carry parasites and viruses, most of them don't affect humans or mammals.

* Sometimes female turkeys will lay their eggs in other turkeys' nests, a practice known as egg dumping. This increases the likelihood that some of the eggs will hatch.

* A mere 24 hours after they've hatched, wild turkey chicks are self-sufficient. They can walk around and even feed themselves!

RESOURCES

Many of the animals in this book are endangered; they need our help. Here are leading organizations dedicated to protecting our planet and its precious wildlife. Get involved and help save your favorite peculiar creatures!

World Wildlife Fund
worldwildlife.org

Oceana
oceana.org

Wildlife Conservation Society
wcs.org

The Sierra Club
sierraclub.org

Conservation International
conservation.org

International Fund for Animal Welfare
ifaw.org

Defenders of Wildlife
defenders.org

International Union for Conservation of Nature
iucn.org

International Animal Rescue
internationalanimalrescue.org

The Nature Conservancy
nature.org

ABOUT THE
AUTHOR

SAMI BAYLY holds a degree in natural history illustration from the University of Newcastle. She's drawn to the weird and wonderful—finding the beauty and importance in all living things, regardless of their appearance—and is eager to share her appreciation with others. She is also the author of *A Curious Collection of Dangerous Creatures* and *A Curious Collection of Wild Companions*. She lives in Newcastle, Australia.

samibayly.com | @samibayly

A CURIOUS COLLECTION OF PECULIAR CREATURES: *An Illustrated Encyclopedia*
Text and illustrations © 2020 by Sami Bayly

Originally published in Australia and New Zealand as *The Illustrated Encyclopaedia of Ugly Animals* by Hachette Australia, an imprint of Hachette Australia Pty Limited, in 2019. First published in North America in revised form by The Experiment, LLC, in 2020.

The Experiment, LLC
220 East 23rd Street, Suite 600
New York, NY 10010-4658
theexperimentpublishing.com

THE EXPERIMENT and its colophon are registered trademarks of The Experiment, LLC. Many of the designations used by manufacturers and sellers to distinguish their products are claimed as trademarks. Where those designations appear in this book and The Experiment was aware of a trademark claim, the designations have been capitalized.

The Experiment's books are available at special discounts when purchased in bulk for premiums and sales promotions as well as for fund-raising or educational use. For details, contact us at info@theexperimentpublishing.com.

Library of Congress Cataloging-in-Publication Data

Names: Bayly, Sami, author.
Title: A curious collection of peculiar creatures : an illustrated
   encyclopedia / Sami Bayly.
Description: New York : The Experiment, 2020. | Originally published in
   Australia and New Zealand as The Illustrated Encyclopaedia of Ugly
   Animals by Hachette Australia, an imprint of Hachette Australia Pty
   Limited, in 2019. | Audience: Ages 8 to 14 | Audience: Grades 4-6
Identifiers: LCCN 2020028882 (print) | LCCN 2020028883 (ebook) | ISBN
   9781615196937 | ISBN 9781615196944 (ebook)
Subjects: LCSH: Animals--Miscellanea--Encyclopedias, Juvenile. | Animal
   behavior--Encyclopedias, Juvenile.
Classification: LCC QL49 .B385 2020 (print) | LCC QL49 (ebook) | DDC
   590.3--dc23
LC record available at https://lccn.loc.gov/2020028882
LC ebook record available at https://lccn.loc.gov/2020028883

ISBN 978-1-61519-693-7
Ebook ISBN 978-1-61519-694-4

Cover design by Jack Dunnington
Text design by Beth Bugler

Manufactured in China

First printing October 2020
10 9 8 7 6 5 4 3